A fine Pastie in Kingsbridge
and 3 books for only
May 29th 2007
Sunny Devon
c/o FJ.

WORLD MOTORCYCLE GUIDE

About this book

With motorcycle sales soaring all over the world, the number of manufacturers and the range of their products is continually increasing. The would-be buyer of a new or second-hand machine is faced with a bewildering selection of motorcycles, each suited to a particular need and aimed at a selected market. WORLD MOTORCYCLE GUIDE lists over 175 machines, complete with a colour photograph and detailed specification of each bike, and should prove invaluable to the first-time purchaser as well as the expert of many years' standing. The choice is enormous, ranging from commuter runabouts like the popular Vespa 125 TS to the super-fast roadburners built by British specialists like Rickman and Dunstall. Competitive riders are also catered for with one-day trials machines from Bultaco and world-championship replica moto-crossers from Suzuki. The pictures and specifications given in this book cover the whole spectrum of motorcycles.

PHOEBUS

Contents

Austria 3
Czechoslovakia 5
Germany 6
Great Britain 13
Italy 17
Japan 37
Spain 52
Sweden 59
U.S.A. 62
U.S.S.R. 64

Made and printed in Great Britain by Purnell and Sons Limited, Paulton (Avon)

ISBN 0 7026 0045 8

KTM Comet GP 125 RS

Engine: 122 cc, single-cylinder two stroke F & S engine. Light alloy wide finned cylinder with chromium-plated lining. Bore and stroke: 54×54 mm. Compression ratio: 11.8:1. Max. power: 17 bhp at 7500 rpm. Bing concentric 28 mm carburettor. Motoplat Thyristor 6V 35-5/18W ignition.

Transmission: primary transmission utilizes gears, secondary transmission utilizes semi-enclosed chain drive. Multiple-disc clutch in oil bath. Six-speed gearbox. Kick start.

Frame: single beam.

Suspension: at front, tele-hydraulic fork; at rear, swinging fork with shock-absorbers.

Wheels: front 2.75×17, rear 3.00×17.

Brakes: 260 mm front and rear.

Tank capacity: 2.6 gallons.

Weight: 226 lbs.

Performance: max. speed 80 mph.

Manufacturer: KTM-Motorfohrzeugbaugesellschaft Kronreif & Trunkenpolz A 5230 Mattighofen

KTM 250/400 MC/GS

Engine: 246 (352) cc, single-cylinder two stroke KTM light alloy cylinder engine. Bore and stroke: 71×62 (81×69) mm. Compression ratio 12:1. Max. power 34 bhp at 7000 (41 at 7900) rpm. Bing carburettor with 36 (38) mm choke. Motoplat Thyristor ignition.

Transmission: primary transmission utilizes gears, secondary transmission utilizes non-enclosed chain drive. Multiple-disc clutch in oil bath. Five-speed gearbox. Kick start.

Frame: duplex cradle.

Suspension: at front, telescopic fork; at rear, swinging fork with shock-absorbers.

Wheels: front 3.00×21, rear 4.50×18.

Brakes: front 180 mm, rear 130 mm.

Tank capacity: 1.7 gallons.

Weight: 195 lbs.

Performance: not stated.

Manufacturer: KTM-Motorfohrzeugbaugesellschaft Kronreif & Trunkenpolz A 5230 Mattighofen

KTM Comet GP 50 RS

Engine: 49 cc, single-cylinder two stroke producing 6.25 bhp at 8000 rpm. Bore and stroke: 38×44 mm. Compression ratio 10:1. 19 mm Bing carburettor. Thyristor ignition.
Transmission: primary transmission by gears, secondary by chain. Multiple-disc clutch in oil bath. Five-speed gearbox. Kick start.
Frame: duplex cradle.
Suspension: at front, telescopic fork; at rear, swinging fork.
Wheels: light alloy wheels 2.50×17 front and rear.
Brakes: 260 mm discs front and rear.
Tank capacity: 2.2 gallons.
Weight: 198 lbs.
Performance: max. speed 52 mph.

Manufacturer: KTM-Motorfohrzeugbaugesellschaft Kronreif & Trunkenpolz, A 5230 Mattighofen

Puch M 50 Jet

Engine: 49.9 cc, single-cylinder two stroke. Bore and stroke: 40×39.7 mm. Compression ratio 11:1. Max. power 6.5 bhp at 8500 rpm. Bing 20 mm carburettor. Bosch flywheel magneto ignition 6V 35/5W with external coil.
Transmission: primary transmission utilizes gears, secondary transmission utilizes semi-enclosed chain drive. Multiple-disc clutch in oil bath. Six-speed gearbox. Kick start.
Frame: single beam with underslung double cradle.
Suspension: at front, telescopic fork; at rear, swinging fork.
Wheels: front 2.50×17, rear 3.50×17.
Brakes: 140 mm front and rear.
Tank capacity: 1.6 gallons.
Weight: 204 lbs.
Performance: max. speed 52 mph.

Manufacturer: Steyr-Daimler-Puch AG, Puchwerke, Graz/ Thondorf

Puch Monza 6 SL

Engine: 49.9 cc, single-cylinder two stroke. Bore and stroke: 40×39.7 mm. Compression ratio 11:1. Max. power not stated. Bing 20 mm carburettor. Bosch 6V 35/5W flywheel magneto ignition with external coil.
Transmission: primary transmission utilizes gears, secondary transmission utilizes non-enclosed chain drive. Multiple-disc clutch in oil bath. Six-speed gearbox. Kick start.
Frame: open duplex cradle.
Suspension: at front, telescopic fork; at rear, swinging fork.
Wheels: front and rear 2.50 ×17.
Brakes: front, hydraulically operated discs, rear, 140 mm drums.
Tank capacity: 1.5 gallons.
Weight: 176 lbs.
Performance: max. speed 58 mph.

Manufacturer: Steyr-Daimler-Puch AG, Puchwerke, Graz/ Thondorf

Puch MC 50 Super

Engine: 49.9 cc single-cylinder two stroke, light alloy cylinder with chromium-plated linings. Bore and stroke: 40×39.7 mm. Compression ratio 14.3:1. Max. power 11.2 bhp at 11,500 rpm. Bing 22 mm carburettor. Bosch electronic ignition.

Transmission: primary transmission utilizes gears, secondary transmission utilizes enclosed chain drive. Multiple-disc clutch in oil bath. Five-speed gearbox. Kick start.
Frame: duplex cradle.
Suspension: at front, telehydraulic fork; at rear, swinging fork.
Wheels: front, 2.50×21, rear, 3.50×18.
Brakes: 125 mm front and rear.
Tank capacity: 1.3 gallons.
Weight: 165 lbs.
Performance: max. speed 47 mph.

Manufacturer: Steyr-Daimler-Puch AG, Puchwerke, Graz/ Thondorf

Puch MC 250 Replica

Engine: 246.3 cc, single-cylinder two stroke, light alloy cylinder with chromium-plated linings. Bore and stroke: 70×64 mm. Compression ratio 12:1. Max. power 43.5 bhp at 8200 rpm. Bing 32 mm carburettor. Bosch electronic ignition.

Transmission: primary transmission utilizes gears, secondary transmission utilizes non-enclosed chain drive. Multiple-disc clutch in oil bath. Five-speed gearbox. Kick start.

Frame: duplex cradle.
Suspension: at front, tele-hydraulic fork; at rear, swinging fork.

Wheels: front 2.75×21, rear 4.50×18.
Brakes: 220 mm front and rear.

Tank capacity: 2 gallons.

Weight: 213 lbs.

Performance: max. speed 77 mph.

Manufacturer: Steyr-Daimler-Puch AG, Puchwerke, Graz/Thondorf

CZ 250

Engine: 246 cc, twin-cylinder two stroke producing 17 bhp at 5250 rpm. Bore and stroke: 52 × 58 mm. Compression ratio 9.3:1. Jikov carburettor with 24 mm choke. Ignition: primary coil, 6V/60W. alternator.

Transmission: primary transmission utilizes chain drive, secondary transmission utilizes semi-enclosed chain drive. Multiple-disc clutch in oil bath. Four-speed gearbox. Kick start.
Frame: tubular single beam.

Suspension: at front, tele-hydraulic fork; at rear, swinging fork.

Wheels: front 3.00×18, rear 3.25×18.

Brakes: 160 mm front and rear.

Tank capacity: 2.8 gallons.

Weight: 310 lbs.

Performance: max. speed 74 mph.

Manufacturer: CZM, Strakonice, Czechoslovakia

Jawa 350 634/6

Engine: 343 cc, twin-cylinder two stroke producing 26 bhp at 5000 rpm. Bore and stroke: 58 ×65 mm. Compression ratio 9.2:1. Jikov carburettor with 26 mm choke. Ignition by battery and coil, 6V/75W. alternator.

Transmission: primary transmission utilizes chain drive, secondary transmission utilizes fully-enclosed chain drive. Multiple-disc clutch in oil bath. Four-speed gearbox. Kick start.
Frame: duplex cradle.

Suspension: at front, tele-hydraulic fork; at rear, swinging fork.

Wheels: front 3.25×18, rear 3.50×18.

Brakes: 160 mm front and rear.

Tank capacity: 3.5 gallons.

Weight: 341 lbs.

Performance: max. speed 83 mph.

Manufacturer: Jawa, Tynec Nad Sazavou, Czechoslovakia

BMW R 90/S

Engine: 898 cc, twin-cylinder four stroke, horizontally opposed cylinders. Bore and stroke: 90×70.6 mm. Compression ratio: 9.5:1. Max. power 67 bhp at 7000 rpm. Two Dell'Orto carburettors with 38 mm choke. Three-phase alternator 180/200. 12V/280W. battery.

Transmission: primary transmission utilizes gears, secondary transmission utilizes prop. shaft and universal couplings. Dry single-plate clutch. Five-speed gearbox. Electric start.

Frame: duplex cradle.

Suspension: at front, telescopic fork; at rear, swinging fork.

Wheels: front 3.25×19, rear 4.00×18.

Brakes: front, twin 200 mm drilled discs, rear, 200 mm.

Tank capacity: 5.2 gallons.

Weight: 473 lbs.

Performance: max. speed 124 mph.

Manufacturer: **Bayerische Motorenwerke AG, 8 Munich, 13 Lerchenauer Strasse 76, West Germany**

BMW R 90/6 – 75/6 – 60/6

Engine: 898 cc (745–599), twin-cyllinder four stroke, horizontally opposed cylinders. Bore & stroke: 90×70.6 mm (82×70.6 – 73.5×70.6). Compression ratio: 9.5:1 (9.2–9). Max. power 60 bhp at 6500 rpm (50-6200 – 40-6400). Two Dell'Orto carburettors with 38 (32-26) mm choke. Three-phase alternator 180-200. 12V/280W. battery.

Transmission: primary transmission utilizes gears, secondary transmission utilizes prop. shaft and universal couplings. Dry single-plate clutch. Five-speed gearbox. Electric start.

Frame: duplex cradle.

Suspension: at front, telescopic fork; at rear, swinging fork.

Wheels: front 3.25×19, rear 4.00×18.

Brakes: front 260 mm drilled discs, rear, 200 mm drum – 90/6 and 75/6. 200 mm drum front and rear – 60/6.

Tank capacity: 3.9 gallons for all 3 models.

Weight: 473 lbs – 90/6 and 75/6. 462 lbs – 60/6.

Performance: max. speed 116 (109-103) mph.

Manufacturer: **Bayerische Motorenwerke AG, 8 Munich, 13 Lerchenauer Strasse 76, West Germany**

Hercules K 125 S

Engine: 122 cc, single-cylinder two stroke. Light-alloy cylinder with a large finning area. Chromium-plated lining. Bore and stroke: 54×54 mm. Compression ratio: 11.8:1. Max. power 17 bhp at 7500 rpm. Central Bing carburettor with 27 mm choke. Motoplat Thyristor 6V 35-5/21W ignition.

Transmission: primary transmission utilizes gears, secondary transmission utilizes semi-enclosed chain drive. Multiple-disc clutch in oil bath. Six-speed gearbox. Kick start.

Frame: duplex cradle.

Suspension: at front, tele-hydraulic fork; at rear, swinging fork.

Wheels: front 2.75×17, rear 3.00×17.

Brakes: front 260 mm disc, rear, 160 mm drum.

Tank capacity: 2.4 gallons.

Weight: 235 lbs.

Performance: max. speed approx. 74 mph.

Manufacturer: Nürnberger Hercules Werke GmbH, 85 Nürnberg, Nopitschstrasse, 70, West Germany

Hercules W 2000

Engine: rotary with contact breaker (F & S/Wankel). Swept volume: 294 cc. Compression ratio 8.5:1. Max. power 26 bhp at 6500 rpm. 32 mm Bing carburettor. Flywheel magneto ignition. 12V/100W alternator.

Transmission: primary transmission utilizes gears, secondary transmission utilizes semi-enclosed chain drive. Multiple-disc clutch in oil bath. Six-speed gearbox. Electric start.

Frame: tubular duplex cradle.

Suspension: at front, Ceriani tele-hydraulic fork; at rear, swinging fork.

Wheels: front 3.00×10, rear 3.25×18.

Brakes: front twin 300 mm discs; rear 180 mm.

Tank capacity: 4 gallons.

Weight: 387 lbs.

Performance: max. speed 86 mph.

Manufacturer: Nürnberger Hercules Werke GmbH, 85 Nürnberg, Nopitschstrasse 70, West Germany

Hercules Sportbike SB 5

Engine: 49 cc, single-cylinder two stroke. Light-alloy cylinder with chromium-plated linings. Bore and stroke: 38×44 mm. Compression ratio 10:1. Max. power 5.3 bhp at 7500 rpm. Bing carburettor with 18 mm choke. Ignition by means of Bosch 6V. 25-4/5W. flywheel magneto. Raised exhaust pipe.

Transmission: primary transmission utlizes gears, secondary transmission utilizes semi-enclosed chain drive. Multiple-disc clutch in oil bath. Five-speed gearbox. Kick start.

Frame: high single beam.

Suspension: at front, tele-hydraulic fork; at rear, swinging fork.

Wheels: front and rear 3.00 ×12.

Brakes: 118 mm front and rear.

Tank capacity: 1.6 gallons.

Weight: 151 lbs.

Performance: max. speed 48 mph.

Manufacturer: Nürnberger Hercules Werke GmbH, 85 Nürnberg, Nopitschstrasse, 70, West Germany

Kreidler Florett RSL (RSHL)

Engine: 50 cc, single-cylinder two stroke. Horizontal light alloy cylinder. Bore and stroke: 40×39.7 mm. Compression ratio 11.3. Max. power 6.25 bhp at 8500 rpm. 20 mm Bing carburettor. Ignition: Bosch 6V, 35–18/5W flywheel magneto.
Transmission: primary transmission utilizes gears, secondary transmission utilizes totally-enclosed chain drive. Multiple-disc clutch in oil bath. Five-speed gearbox.
Frame: tubular single beam.

Suspension: at front, tele-hydraulic fork; at rear, swinging fork.

Wheels: front and rear 2.75×17.

Brakes: 160 mm front and rear.

Tank capacity: 2.6 gallons.

Weight: 182 lbs.

Performance: max. speed 52 mph.

Manufacturer: Kreidler-Werke GmbH, Fahrzeugwerke, 7014 Kornwestheim, West Germany

Kreidler Mustang Cross

Engine: 50 cc, single-cylinder two stroke producing 6.25 bhp at 8500 rpm. Horizontal light alloy cylinder. Bore and stroke: 40×39.7 mm. Compression ratio 10:1. BING 20 mm carburettor. Bosch 6V, 18/5W flywheel magneto ignition.

Transmission: primary transmission utilizes gears, secondary transmission utilizes totally enclosed chain drive. Multiple-disc clutch in oil bath. Five-speed gearbox.

Frame: tubular single beam.

Suspension: at front, tele-hydraulic fork; at rear, swinging fork with pneumatic shock-absorbers.

Wheels: front 2.50×19, rear 2.75×17.

Brakes: 120 mm front and rear.

Tank capacity: 2.6 gallons.

Weight: 180 lbs.

Performance: max. speed 52 mph.

Manufacturer: Kreidler Werke GmbH, Fahrzeugwerke, 7014 Kornwestheim, West Germany

Maico MD 50

Engine: 49 cc, single-cylinder two stroke. Bore and stroke: 38×44 mm. Compression ratio 11.2:1. Max. power 6.3 bhp at 8200 rpm. Bing 20 mm carburettor. Flywheel magneto ignition with external coil 6V 35-18/5W.
Transmission: primary transmission utilizes gears, secondary transmission utilizes semi-enclosed chain drive. Multiple-disc clutch in oil bath. Six-speed gearbox. Kick start.
Frame: duplex cradle.
Suspension: at front, telescopic fork; at rear, swinging fork.
Wheels: front 2.50×16, rear 3.00×16.
Brakes: 136 mm front and rear.
Tank capacity: 2.9 gallons.
Weight: 201 lbs.
Performance: max. speed 52 mph.

Manufacturer: Maico Fahrzeugfabrik GmbH, 7403 Pfäffingen/Tüb, West Germany

Maico MD 125

Engine: 124 cc, single-cylinder two stroke. Light alloy cylinders. Bore and stroke: 54×54 mm. Compression ratio 11:1. Max. power 16 bhp at 7800 rpm. Bing carburettor with 26 mm choke. Flywheel magneto ignition with external coil 6V 35-18/5W.
Transmission: primary by gears, secondary by semi-enclosed chain drive. Multiple-disc clutch in oil bath. Six-speed gearbox. Kick start.
Frame: duplex cradle.
Suspension: at front, telehydraulic fork, at rear, swinging fork with shock-absorbers.
Wheels: front, 2.50-16 and rear 3.00×16.
Brakes: 136 mm front and rear.
Tank capacity: 2.9 gallons.
Weight: 217 lbs.
Performance: max. speed 77 mph.

Manufacturer: Maico Fahrzeugfabrik GmbH, 7403 Pfäffingen/Tüb, West Germany

Maico MC (GS) 400/450

Engine: 386 (454) cc, single-cylinder two stroke. Light alloy wide finned cylinder. Bore and stroke: 77×83 (82×83) mm. Compression ratio 12:1. Max. power 43 bhp at 7000 rpm. (47 bhp at 6800 rpm.) Bing concentric 36 mm carburettor. MC engine with APPT magneto ignition.

Transmission: primary transmission utilizes Triplex chain drive, secondary transmission utilizes non-enclosed chain drive. Five-speed gearbox. Kick start.

Frame: duplex cradle.

Suspension: at front, telehydraulic fork; at rear, swinging fork.

Wheels: front, 3.00×21, rear 4.50×18.

Brakes: front 160 mm, rear 136 mm.

Tank capacity: 1.5 gallons.

Weight: 213 (217) lbs.

Performance: not stated.

Manufacturer: Maico Fahrzeugfabrik GmbH, 7403 Pfäffingen/Tüb, West Germany

Münch 4 – 1200 TTS/TTS E

Engine: 1177 cc, NSU four-cylinder four stroke, air-cooled, transverse assembly. Bore and stroke: 75×66.6 mm. Compression ratio 8.5:1. Max. power 88 bhp at 6000 rpm. Two horizontal 40 mm Weber carburettors. Forced lubrication of gears. Coil ignition and on request Bosch transistorized ignition. 12V/180W alternator.

Transmission: primary transmission utilizes helical gears, secondary transmission utilizes enclosed chain drive. Multiple-dry-disc clutch. Four-speed gearbox. Electric start.

Frame: duplex cradle.

Suspension: at front, Ceriani or Rickman fork; at rear, swinging fork with adjustable shock-absorbers.

Wheels: front 3.25×19, rear 4.00 per 18.

Brakes: twin 250 mm front and rear.

Tank capacity: 7.4 gallons.

Weight: 655 lbs.

Performance: max. speed 136 mph.

Manufacturer: Heinz W. Henke, 6472 Altenstadt, Hegwaldstrasse 2, West Germany

MZ TS 250

Engine: 243 cc, single-cylinder two stroke with resilient mountings producing 21 bhp at 5900 rpm. Bore and stroke 69×65 mm. Compression ratio 10:1. Carburettor with central float chamber. Ignition utilizes 6V – 12A – 40–45W battery and induction coil.

Transmission: primary transmission utilizes chain drive, secondary transmission utilizes fully - enclosed chain drive. Four-speed gearbox.

Frame: reinforced supporting framework.

Suspension: at front, tele-hydraulic fork; at rear, swinging fork.

Wheels: front 3.00×16, rear 3.50×16.

Brakes: front 160 mm, rear 160 mm.

Tank capacity: 3.75 gallons.

Weight: 286 lbs.

Performance: max. speed 80 mph.

Manufacturer: VEB Motorradwerk Zschopau, Zschopau/Erzgebirge, East Germany

Simson S 50 BI

Engine: 49 cc, single-cylinder two stroke with chromium-plated light-alloy cylinders. Bore and stroke: 40×39.5 mm. Compression ratio: 9.5:1. Max. power 3.8 bhp at 5500 rpm. Carburettor with 19 mm choke. Ignition: 6V – 25/4/5W flywheel magneto.

Transmission: primary transmission utilizes gears, secondary transmission utilizes semi-enclosed chain drive. Multiple-disc clutch in oil bath. Three-speed gearbox. Kick start.

Frame: tubular single beam.

Suspension: at front, telehydraulic fork; at rear, swinging fork with shock-absorbers.

Wheels: front and rear 2.75×20.

Brakes: 125 mm front and rear.

Tank capacity: 2 gallons.

Weight: 171 lbs.

Performance: max. speed 37 mph.

Manufacturer: IFA-Kombinat VEB Fahrzeug- und Jagdwaffenwerk Ernst Thälmann, Suhl/Thur, East Germany

Zündapp MC 125

Engine: 123 cc, single-cylinder two stroke, producing 21 bhp at 8500 rpm. Wide finned cylinder of light alloy with chromium-plated lining. Bore and stroke: 54×54 mm. Compression ratio 11.3:1. Bing concentric 28 mm carburettor. Because of the exhaust arrangement the machine is not suitable for use on public roads.
Transmission: primary transmission utilizes gears, secondary transmission utilizes semi-enclosed chain drive. Multiple-disc clutch in oil bath. Five-speed gearbox.
Frame: duplex cradle.
Suspension: at front, telehydraulic fork; at rear, swinging fork.
Wheels: front 3.00×21, rear 3.75×18.
Brakes: 150 mm front and rear.
Tank capacity: 1.5 gallons.
Weight: 187 lbs.
Performance: not stated.

Manufacturer: Zündapp Werke GmbH, 8 Munich 80, Anzinger Str. 1–3, West Germany

Zündapp GS 125 Special Competition

Engine: 123 cc, single-cylinder two stroke producing 20 bhp at 8000 rpm. Wide finned cylinder of light alloy with chromium-plated lining. Bore and stroke: 54×54 mm. Compression ratio 11.3:1. 28 mm concentric Bing carburettor. Bosch Thyristor 6V 35-5/18W ignition with external coil.
Transmission: primary transmission utilizes gears, secondary transmission utilizes semi-enclosed chain drive. Multiple-disc clutch in oil bath. Five-speed gearbox. Kick start.
Frame: duplex cradle.
Suspension: at front, telehydraulic fork; at rear, swinging fork.
Wheels: front, 3.00×21, rear, 3.75×18.
Brakes: 150 mm front and rear.
Tank capacity: 2.2 gallons.
Weight: 198 lbs.
Performance: max. speed 74 mph.

Manufacturer: Zündapp Werke GmbH, 8 Munich 80, Anzinger Str. 1–3, West Germany

Zündapp KS 50 water-cooled

Engine: 49 cc, single-cylinder two-stroke water-cooled with chrome liner. Light alloy cylinder. Bore and stroke: 39× 41.8 mm. Compression ratio 11: 1. Max. power 6.25 bhp at 8400 rpm. Bing carburettor with 19 mm choke. Bosch Thyristor ignition 6V 25W–4/5W.

Transmission: primary by gears, secondary transmission by enclosed chain. Multiple-disc clutch in oil bath. Five-speed gearbox. Kick start.

Frame: central cradle.

Suspension: at front, tele-hydraulic fork; at rear, swinging fork.

Wheels: front and rear 2.75× 21.

Brakes: 150 mm front and rear.

Tank capacity: 2.4 gallons.

Weight: 184 lbs.

Performance: max. speed 52 mph.

Manufacturer: Zündapp-Werke GmbH, 8 München 80, Anzinger Str. 1-3., West Germany

Zündapp KS 125 Super Sport

Engine: 123.6 cc, single-cylinder two stroke producing 17 bhp at 7600 rpm. Wide finned light alloy cylinder with chromium-plated lining. Bore and stroke: 54×54 mm. Compression ratio 12.4:1. Bing concentric 27 mm carburettor. Bosch Thyristor contactless ignition, 6V 35-5/18W with external coil.

Transmission: primary transmission utilizes gears, secondary transmission utilizes semi-enclosed chain drive. Multiple-disc clutch in oil bath. Five -speed gearbox. Kick start.

Frame: duplex cradle.

Suspension: at front, tele-hydraulic fork; at rear, swinging fork.

Wheels: front 2.75×18, rear 3.25×18.

Brakes: 150 mm front and rear.

Tank capacity: 3 gallons.

Weight: 242 lbs.

Performance: max. speed 74 mph.

Manufacturer: Zündapp-Werke GmbH, 8 München 80, Anzinger Str. 1-3., West Germany

Dunstall Suzuki 750

Engine: 738 cc, three-cylinder, two stroke, water cooled with pump, thermostatic control and fan for idling. Bore and stroke: 70×64 mm. Compression ratio: 6.9:1. Max. power 70 bhp at 6500 rpm. Three Mikuni carburettors with 40 mm choke. Forced lubrication. Ignition by means of battery and induction coil. 12V/280W alternator.
Transmission: primary transmission by gears secondary by semi-enclosed chain drive. Multiple-disc clutch in oil bath. Five-speed gearbox. Electric start.
Frame: duplex cradle.
Suspension: at front, telescopic fork; at rear, swinging fork with shock absorbers.
Wheels: front 3.25×19, rear 4.00×18.
Brakes: front, 295 mm discs, rear, duplex 180 mm drums.
Tank capacity: 3.7 gallons.
Weight: 470 lbs.
Performance: max. speed 133 mph.

Manufacturer: Paul Dunstall Organisation Ltd., Crabtree Manorway, Belvedere, Kent

Dunstall Honda 900

Engine: 899 cc, four-cylinder four stroke, overhead valve engine driven by camshaft and rocker arms. Bore and stroke: 67×63 mm. Compression ratio 10:1. Max. power 72 bhp at 8000 rpm. Two Keihin 28 mm carburettors. Battery ignition, 12V/210W alternator.

Transmission: primary transmission utilizes chain drive, secondary transmission utilizes semi-enclosed chain drive. Multiple-disc clutch in oil bath. Five-speed gearbox.
Frame: duplex cradle.
Suspension: at front, telehydraulic fork; at rear, swinging fork.
Wheels: front 3.60×19, rear 4.10×19.
Brakes: front, twin 175 mm discs rear, 175 mm drum.
Tank capacity: 3.9 gallons.
Weight: 468 lbs.
Performance: max. speed approx. 124 mph.

Manufacturer: Paul Dunstall Organisation Ltd., Crabtree Manorway, Belvedere, Kent

Dunstall Kawasaki 1100

Engine: 1098 cc, four-cylinder four stroke overhead-valve engine driven by camshaft. Bore and stroke: 72.8×66 mm. Compression ratio 10:1. Max. power 86 bhp at 7800 rpm. Four Mikuni carburettors 28 mm in diameter. Ignition by means of battery and induction coil. 12V alternator.

Transmission: primary transmission utilizes gears, secondary transmission utilizes semi-enclosed chain drive. Multiple-disc clutch in oil bath. Five-speed gearbox. Electric/Kick start.

Frame: duplex cradle.

Suspension: at front, telescopic fork; at rear, swinging fork with adjustable shock-absorbers.

Wheels: front 3.60×19, rear 4.10×19.

Brakes: front, 296 mm hydraulic discs, rear, 200 mm drum.

Tank capacity: 4.4 gallons.

Weight: 462 lbs.

Performance: max. speed 136 mph.

Manufacturer: Paul Dunstall Organisation Ltd., Crabtree Manorway, Belvedere, Kent

Greeves Griffon Mark II 380 cc

Engine: 380 cc, single-cylinder two stroke producing 44 bhp at 6750 rpm. Compression ratio 13.5:1. Mikuni 34 mm carburettor. Motoplat Thyristor ignition. 6V/60W electrical system.

Transmission: primary transmission utilizes gears, secondary transmission utilizes semi-enclosed chain drive. Multiple-disc clutch in oil bath. Four-speed gearbox. Kick start.

Frame: duplex cradle.

Suspension: at front, tele-hydraulic fork, at rear, swinging fork with shock-absorbers.

Wheels: front 3.00×21, rear 4.50×18.

Brakes: 150 mm front and rear.

Tank capacity: 1.4 gallons.

Weight: 237 lbs.

Performance: not stated.

Manufacturer: Greeves Motorcycles, Armstrong Road, Benfleet, Essex

Norton Commando MK 3

Engine: 828 cc, twin-cylinder four stroke (Twin), overhead valve driven by rocker arms and push rods. Bore and stroke: 77×89 mm. Compression ratio 8.5:1. Max. power 58 bhp at 5900 rpm. Two Amal concentric carburettors. Forced lubrication. Ignition by means of Lucas transistorized battery 12V/150W alternator—2 coils.

Transmission: primary transmission utilizes Triplex chain drive, secondary transmission utilizes semi-enclosed chain drive. Multiple-disc clutch in oil bath. Four-speed gearbox. Electric start.

Frame: duplex cradle. Engine mounted on 3 special resilient mountings so as to avoid vibration.

Suspension: at front, telescopic fork; at rear, swinging fork.

Wheels: front and rear 4.10×19.

Brakes: 270 mm front and rear.

Tank capacity: 6.3 gallons.

Weight: 466 lbs.

Performance: max. speed 117 mph.

Manufacturer: Norton Triumph Ltd, North Way, Andover, Hampshire SP10 5BD

Rickman Honda 750 CR/CR Sport

Manufacturer: Rickman Brothers (Engineering) Ltd, Stem Lane, New Milton, Hants

Engine: 736 cc, four-cylinder four stroke, overhead valve. Bore and stroke: 61×63 mm. Compression ratio 9:1. Max. power 67 bhp at 8000 rpm. Ignition by means of 12V 18 Ah battery induction coil. Forced lubrication at trocoidal tubes.

Transmission: primary transmission utilizes dual Simplex chain drive, secondary transmission utilizes semi-enclosed chain drive. Multiple-disc clutch in oil bath. Five-speed gearbox. Electric/Kick start.

Frame: duplex cradle.

Suspension: at front, telehydraulic fork; at rear, swinging fork.

Wheels: front, 3.25×19, rear, 4.00×18.

Brakes: front 296 mm disc, rear 180 mm drum.

Tank capacity: 3.9 gallons.

Weight: 495 lbs.

Performance: max. speed 130 mph.

Rickman Kawasaki 900 CR/CR Sport

Manufacturer: Rickman Brothers (Engineering) Ltd, Stem Lane, New Milton, Hants

Engine: 903 cc, four-cylinder four stroke engine, overhead valve driven by 2 camshafts. Bore and stroke: 66×66 mm. Compression ratio 8.5:1. Max. power 82 bhp at 8500 rpm. Four Mikuni carburettors 24 mm in diameter. Ignition by means of battery and induction coil, 12V alternator.

Transmission: primary transmission utilizes gears, secondary transmission utilizes semi-enclosed chain drive. Multiple-disc clutch in oil bath. Five-speed gearbox. Electric/Kick start.

Frame: duplex cradle.

Suspension: at front, telescopic fork; at rear, swinging fork with adjustable shock-absorbers.

Wheels: front 3.25×19, rear 4.00×18.

Brakes: front 296 mm disc, rear 200 mm brake.

Tank capacity: 3.9 gallons.

Weight: 528 lbs.

Performance: max. speed over 124 mph.

Triumph Tiger 750

Engine: 744 cc, twin-cylinder transverse four stroke, light alloy head, single camshaft. Bore and stroke: 76×82 mm. Compression ratio 7.9:1. Max. power not stated. Amal Concentric carburettor. Battery ignition with coil. 12V/120W alternator.

Transmission: primary transmission utilizes triplex chain drive, secondary transmission utilizes semi-enclosed chain drive. Clutch in oil bath. Five-speed gearbox foot-operated. Kick start.

Frame: duplex cradle.

Suspension: at front, telehydraulic fork; at rear, swinging fork with adjustable shock-absorbers.

Wheels: front 3.25×19 and rear 4.00×18.

Brakes: 254 mm discs front and rear.

Tank capacity: 4 gallons.

Weight: 413 lbs.

Performance: max. speed 105 mph.

Manufacturer: Norton Triumph Ltd, North Way, Andover, Hampshire SP10 5BD

Triumph Trident T 160

Engine: 740 cc, three-cylinder transverse four stroke, light alloy head and cylinders, "High Performance" camshaft. Bore and stroke: 67×70 mm. Compression ratio 9.5:1. Max. power 58 bhp at 7250 rpm. Three Amal Concentric 27 mm carburettors. Battery ignition with three coils. 12V/120W alternator.

Transmission: primary transmission utilizes duplex chain drive, secondary transmission utilizes semi-enclosed chain drive. Dry, single-disc clutch. Five-speed gearbox. Electric start.

Frame: tubular.

Suspension: at front, telehydraulic fork; at rear, swinging fork with adjustable shock-absorbers.

Wheels: 4.10×19 front and rear.

Brakes: 254 mm front and rear.

Tank capacity: 4.8 gallons.

Weight: 503 lbs.

Performance: max. speed 117 mph.

Manufacturer: Norton Triumph Ltd, North Way, Andover, Hampshire SP10 5BD

Agrati-Garelli Cross KL 50 4 V

Engine: 49.6 cc, single-cylinder two stroke producing 1.5 bhp at 4800 rpm. Bore and stroke: 40×39.6 mm. Compression ratio 8:1. Dell'Orto carburettor, type: SHB 18/12 B. Electronic 6V/18W flywheel magneto ignition.
Transmission: primary transmission utilizes gears secondary transmission utilizes chain drive. Multiple-disc clutch in oil bath. Four-speed gearbox. Kick start.
Frame: duplex cradle.
Suspension: at front, telescopic fork; at rear, telescopic adjustable shock-absorbers.
Wheels: front 2.50×19, rear 2.50×17.
Brakes: hubs incorporating drum brakes.
Tank capacity: 2.5 gallons.
Weight: 149 lbs.
Performance: max. speed 24 mph.

Manufacturer: Agrati-Garelli, Monticello B. (Como).

Agrati-Garelli KL 50 E Cross 5 V

Engine: as for KL 50 4 V.
Transmission: as for KL 50 4 V but with five-speed gearbox.
Frame: duplex cradle.
Suspension: at front, tele-hydraulic fork; at rear, adjustable tele-hydraulic shock-absorbers with 3 load positions.
Wheels: front 2.50×19, rear 3.00×17.
Brakes: not stated.
Tank capacity: 2.2 gallons.
Weight: 167 lbs.
Performance: max. speed 24 mph.

Manufacturer: Agrati-Garelli, Monticello B. (Como).

AMF Harley-Davidson SS 175

Engine: 174.15 cc, single-cylinder two stroke producing 15.5 bhp at 6750 rpm. Bore and stroke 61×59.6 mm. Compression ratio 10.7:1. Dell'Orto VHB 27 AD carburettor. Induction coil ignition 12V alternator. Battery 18Ah.
Transmission: primary transmission utilizes helical gears, secondary transmission utilizes single chain drive. Dry multiple-disc clutch. Five-speed gearbox. Kick start.
Frame: duplex cradle.
Suspension: at front, telescopic hydraulic fork; at rear, hydraulic shock-absorbers.
Wheels: front 3.25×19, rear 4.00×18.
Brakes: 180 mm front and rear.
Tank capacity: 2.8 gallons.
Weight: 253 lbs.
Performance: max. speed 68 mph.

Manufacturer: AMF Harley-Davidson Varese S.p.A. 21100 Schiranna (VA).

AMF Harley-Davidson SX 175

Engine: as for AMF Harley-Davidson SS 175. Max. power 17 bhp at 7500 rpm. Flywheel ignition, electronic alternator, discharge capacitor, 12V battery.
Transmission: as for SS 175. Multiple-disc clutch in oil bath. Five-speed gearbox with foot control. Kick start.
Frame: duplex cradle.
Suspension: at front, telescopic hydraulic fork; at rear, 5 position hydraulic shock-absorbers.

Wheels: front 3.00×19, rear 3.50×18
Brakes: ·140 mm front and rear.
Tank capacity: 2.3 gallons.
Weight: 242 lbs.
Performance: max. speed 68 mph.

Manufacturer: AMF Harley-Davidson Varese S.p.A. 21100 Schiranna (VA).

AMF Harley-Davidson SX 250

Engine: 242.6 cc, single-cylinder two stroke producing 23 bhp at 7750 rpm. Bore and stroke: 72×59.6 mm. Compression ratio 10.3:1. Dell'Orto PHB 32AD carburettor. Lubrication by means of pump operation utilizing a separate mixture. Flywheel ignition, electronic alternator with discharge capacitor, 12V battery.
Transmission: primary transmission utilizes helical gears, secondary transmission utilizes single chain drive. Multiple-disc clutch in oil bath. Five-speed gearbox. Kick start.
Frame: duplex cradle.
Suspension: at front, telescopic hydraulic fork; at rear, 5 position hydraulic shock-absorbers and external helical springs.
Wheels: front 3.00×21, rear 4.00×18.
Brakes: 140 mm front and rear.
Tank capacity: 2.3 gallons.
Weight: 253 lbs.
Performance: max. speed 74 mph.

Manufacturer: AMF Harley-Davidson Varese S.p.A. 21100 Schiranna (VA)

AMF Harley-Davidson RR 250

Engine: 248 cc, twin-cylinder two stroke. Bore and stroke: 56×50 mm. Compression ratio 11.3:1. Max. power not stated. Dell'Orto 34 mm carburettors. Forced lubrication. Dansi CDI ignition.

Transmission: primary transmission utilizes helical gears, secondary transmission utilizes single chain drive. Dry multiple-disc clutch. Six-speed gearbox. Push start.

Frame: duplex cradle.

Suspension: at front, telescopic hydraulic fork; at rear, hydraulic shock-absorbers.

Wheels: front 3.00×18, rear 3.25×18.
Tank capacity: 6.1 gallons.

Brakes: front disc, rear drum.
Weight: 226 lbs.

Performance: not stated.

Manufacturer: AMF Harley-Davidson Varese S.p.A. 21100 Schiranna (VA)

AMF Harley-Davidson SST 250

Engine: 242.6 cc, single-cylinder two stroke producing 20.5 bhp at 7200 rpm. Bore and stroke: 72×59 mm. Compression ratio 10.3:1. Dell'Orto PHB 32 AD carburettor. Ignition by means of induction coil, 12V 18Ah alternator.

Transmission: primary transmission utilizes helical gears, secondary transmission utilizes chain drive. Dry multiple-disc clutch. Five-speed gearbox. Kick start.

Frame: duplex cradle.

Suspension: at front, telehydraulic fork; at rear, swinging fork with shock-absorbers.

Wheels: front 3.25×19, rear 4.00×18.

Brakes: front 220 mm disc, rear 180 mm drum.

Tank capacity: 2.8 gallons.

Weight: 259 lbs.

Performance: max. speed 83 mph.

Manufacturer: AMF Harley-Davidson Varese S.p.A. 21100 Schiranna (VA)

Aspes Navaho 50 CRS

Engine: 49 cc, single-cylinder two stroke producing 12.2 bhp at 12,800 rpm. Bore and stroke: 39.5×40 mm. Compression ratio 12.5:1. Dell'Orto carburettor. Electronic Motoplat ignition.
Transmission: primary transmission by gears, secondary by chain. Multiple-disc clutch in oil bath. Six-speed gearbox. Kick start.
Frame: duplex cradle.
Suspension: at front, telehydraulic fork; at rear, swinging fork with shock-absorbers.
Wheels: front 2.50×21, rear 3.50×18.
Brakes: drum brakes front and rear.
Tank capacity: 1.8 gallons.
Weight: 149 lbs.
Performance: not stated.

Manufacturer: Sorrentino T&C, Fabbrica Moto Aspes, Via Magenta, 29 Gallarate (Varese)

Aspes Navaho CS Special

Engine: 49 cc, single-cylinder two stroke. Bore and stroke: 38.8×42 mm. Max. power not stated. 9 mm Dell'Orto carburettor. Electronic 6V/18W ignition.
Transmission: primary transmission by gears, secondary by chain. Multiple-disc clutch in oil bath. Six-speed gearbox. Kick start.
Frame: duplex cradle.
Suspension: at front, telehydraulic fork; at rear, swinging fork.
Wheels: front 2.50×21, rear 3.50×18.
Brakes: drum front and rear.
Tank capacity: 1.8 gallons.
Weight: 154 lbs.
Performance: max. speed not stated.

Manufacturer: Sorrentino T & C, Fabbrica Moto Aspes, Via Magenta 29, Gallarate (Varese)

Aspes Hopi 125 RGS

Engine: 123 cc, single-cylinder two stroke producing 24.6 bhp at 9800 rpm. Bore and stroke: 54×54 mm. Compression ratio 11.5:1. 30 mm Dell'Orto carburettor. Motoplat 6V/35W ignition.
Transmission: primary transmission by gears, secondary by chain. Multiple-disc clutch in oil bath. Five-speed gearbox. Kick start.
Frame: duplex cradle.
Suspension: at front, telehydraulic fork; at rear, swinging fork with gas dampers.
Wheels: front 3.00×21, rear 4.00×18.
Brakes: drum front and rear.
Tank capacity: 2 gallons.
Weight: 209 lbs.
Performance: max. speed not stated.

Manufacturer: Sorrentino T & C, Fabbrica Moto Aspes, Via Magenta 29 Gallarate (Varese)

Aspes 125 CRS

Engine: 123 cc, single-cylinder two stroke producing 24 bhp at 9500 rpm. Bore and stroke: 54 ×54 mm. Compression ratio 12.5:1. 34 mm carburettor. Electronic Motoplat ignition.
Transmission: primary transmission by gears, secondary by chain. Multiple-disc clutch in oil bath. Five-speed gearbox. Kick start.
Frame: duplex cradle.
Suspension: at front, telehydraulic fork; at rear, shock-absorbers.
Wheels: front 3.00×21, rear 4.00×18.
Brakes: drum front and rear.
Tank capacity: not stated.
Weight: 198 lbs.
Performance: max. speed not stated.

Manufacturer: Sorrentino T&C, Fabbrica Moto Aspes, Via Magenta, 29 Gallarate (Varese)

Aspes Juma 125

Engine: 123 cc, single-cylinder two stroke. Bore and stroke: 54 ×54 mm. Compression ratio 11.5:1. Max. power 20 bhp at 9500rpm. 30 mm Dell'Orto carburettor. Motoplat 6V/35W ignition.
Transmission: primary transmission by gears, secondary by chain. Multiple-disc clutch in oil bath. Five-speed gearbox. Kick start.

Frame: duplex cradle.
Suspension: at front, telehydraulic fork; at rear, swinging fork.
Wheels: front 2.50×18, rear 3.00×18.
Brakes: front disc, rear drum.
Tank capacity: 2 gallons.
Weight: 187 lbs.
Performance: max. speed 89 mph.

Manufacturer: Sorrentino T & C, Fabbrica Moto Aspes, Via Magenta 29, Gallarate (Varese)

Benelli 125 2C Elettronica

Engine: 125 cc, twin-cylinder two-stroke producing 16 bhp at 7800 rpm. Bore and stroke: 42.5×44 mm. Compression ratio: 10:1. Twin Dell'Orto carburettors. Electronic ignition. Electrics 6V 9 Ah.
Transmission: primary transmission by gears, secondary by chain. Multiple-disc clutch in oil bath. Five-speed gearbox. Kick start.

Frame: duplex cradle.
Suspension: telescopic with shock-absorbers.
Wheels: front 2.75×18, rear 3.00×18.
Brakes: 260 mm front, 158 mm rear.
Tank capacity: 2.75 gallons.
Weight: 253 lbs.
Performance: max. speed approx. 74 mph.

Manufacturer: F.lli Benelli S.p.A., Via Mameli 22, Pesaro

Benelli 500 Four

Engine: 498.5 cc, four-cylinder four stroke producing 55 bhp at 9800 rpm. Overhead valve. Bore and stroke: 56×50.6 mm. Compression ratio: 10.2:1. Ignition by means of induction coil and 12V 15Ah battery.

Transmission: primary transmission by central chain drive and lateral gear drive, secondary transmission utilizes semi-enclosed chain drive. Multiple-disc clutch in oil bath. Five-speed gearbox. Electric/Kick start.

Frame: duplex cradle.

Suspension: at front, telehydraulic fork; at rear, swinging fork.

Wheels: front 3.50×18, rear 4.10×18.

Brakes: front 280 mm disc rear,

Tank capacity: 4.8 gallons.

Weight: 418 lbs.

Performance: max. speed 117 mph.

Manufacturer: Fratelli Benelli S.p.A., Via Mameli 22, Pesaro

Benelli 250 Café Racer

Engine: 231.4 cc twin-cylinder two stroke. Bore and stroke: 56×47 mm. Compression ratio 10:1. Max. power not stated. Dell'Orto VHB 25 BS carburettors. Flywheel magneto ignition, coil, 12V/130W alternator.
Transmission: primary transmission utilizes gears, secondary transmission utilizes semi-enclosed chain drive. Multiple-disc clutch in oil bath. Five-speed gearbox. Kick start.
Frame: duplex cradle.
Suspension: at front, telehydraulic fork; at rear, swinging fork.
Wheels: front 3.00×18, rear 3.25×18.
Brakes: front twin discs hydraulically operated, rear brake 158 mm.
Tank capacity: 2.9 gallons.
Weight: 242 lbs.
Performance: max. speed 99 mph.

Manufacturer: Fratelli Benelli S.p.A., Via Mameli 22, Pesaro

Benelli 250 Four

Engine: 231 cc, four-cylinder four stroke producing 26.6 bhp at 10,500 rpm. Bore and stroke: 44×38 mm. Compression ratio: 11.5:1. Four carburettors. Ignition by means of battery and induction coil. 12V/100W alternator.
Transmission: primary transmission utilizes toothed chain drive, secondary transmission utilizes semi-enclosed chain drive. Multiple-disc clutch in oil bath. Five-speed gearbox. Electric/Kick start.
Frame: tubular.
Suspension: at front, telehydraulic fork; at rear, swinging fork.
Wheels: front 3.00×18, rear 3.25×18.
Brakes: front, disc brakes hydraulically operated, rear, 158 mm drum.
Tank capacity: 2.5 gallons.
Weight: 257 lbs.
Performance: max. speed 93 mph.

Manufacturer: Fratelli Benelli S.p.A., Via Mameli 22, Pesaro

Benelli 750 Six

Engine: 747.7 cc, six-cylinder four stroke, single overhead camshaft driven by a central chain. Bore and stroke: 50×50.6 mm. Compression ratio 9:1. Max. power 75 bhp at 9000 rpm. Three Dell'Orto VHB 24 carburettors. Induction coil ignition with external coils, 12V 15Ah battery.

Transmission: primary transmission by chain, secondary transmission utilizes chain drive. Multiple-disc clutch in oil bath. Five-speed gearbox. Electric/Kick start.

Frame: duplex cradle.

Suspension: at front, telescopic fork; at rear, swinging fork with adjustable shock-absorbers.

Wheels: front, 3.50×18, rear, 4.25×18.

Brakes: front twin hydraulically operated 280 mm discs, 200 mm drum rear brake.

Tank capacity: 4.8 gallons.

Weight: 484 lbs.

Performance: max. speed approx. 124 mph.

Manufacturer: Fratelli Benelli S.p.A., Via Mameli 22, Pesaro

Benelli 250 2C Elettronica

Engine: 232 cc, twin-cylinder two-stroke producing 30 bhp at 8000 rpm. Bore and stroke: 56×47 mm. Compression ratio: 10:1. Twin Dell'Orto VHB 25 BS/BD carburettors. Ignition by flywheel magneto. Electrics 6V 9 Ah.

Transmission: primary transmission by gears, secondary by chain. Multiple-disc clutch in oil bath. Five-speed gearbox. Kick start.

Frame: duplex cradle.
Suspension: telescopic with shock-absorbers.

Wheels: front 3.00×18, rear 3.25×18.
Brakes: 260 mm front, 158 mm rear.

Tank capacity: 2.75 gallons.
Weight: 303 lbs.

Performance: max. speed approx. 86 mph.

Manufacturer: F.lli Benelli SpA, Via Mameli 22, Pesaro

Cimatti Mini Chic VI

Engine: 49 cc, single-cylinder two stroke, horizontally mounted. Dell'Orto carburettor. 6V/18W electrical system. Ignition by flywheel magneto 6V/18W.

Transmission: automatic clutch with single gear and pedal start.

Frame: tubular beam.

Suspension: at front, telescopic fork: at rear, swinging fork.

Wheels: 3.00×10 front and rear.
Brakes: drum front and rear.

Tank capacity: 0.6 gallons.
Weight: 97 lbs.
Performance: not stated.

Manufacturer: Cimatti, Pioppe de Salvaro (Bologna)

Cimatti Kaiman Trial 50 cc 6M

Engine: 49 cc, single-cylinder two-stroke. Bore and stroke: 40×39 mm. Compression ratio 7:1. Max. power 12 bhp at 7000 rpm. Dell'Orto carburettor. Ignition: fly-wheel magneto 6V/18W.

Transmission: multiple-disc clutch. Six-speed gearbox. Kick start.

Frame: duplex cradle.

Suspension: at front, telescopic fork; at rear swinging fork.

Wheels: front 2.50×19, rear 3.00×17.

Brakes: 118 mm front and rear.

Tank capacity: 1.7 gallons.

Weight: 165 lbs.

Performance: max. speed not stated.

Manufacturer: Cimatti Marco, Pioppe di Salvaro (Bologna)

Ducati 125 Regolarità

Engine: 123.7 cc, single-cylinder two stroke. Bore and stroke: 54×54 mm. Compression ratio 10.5:1. Max. power not stated. Dell'Orto PHB carburettor with central float chamber, 30 mm choke.

Transmission: primary transmission utilizes gears, secondary transmission utilizes semi-enclosed chain drive. Multiple-disc clutch in oil bath. Six-speed gearbox.

Frame: duplex cradle.
Suspension: at front, telescopic fork; at rear, swinging fork with shock-absorbers.

Wheels: front 3.00×21, rear 3.75×18.
Brakes: front, 125 mm, rear, 140 mm.
Tank capacity: 1.3 gallons.
Weight: 237 lbs.

Performance: max. speed 74 mph.

Manufacturer: Ducati Meccanica S.p.A., Via Ducati 3, Bologna

Ducati 750 SS

Engine: 748 cc, twin-cylinder arranged longitudinally in 90° V configuration. Four stroke. Positive timing. Bore and stroke: 80 ×74.4 mm. Compression ratio: 9.5:1. Max. power 72 bhp at 9500 rpm. Two Dell'Orto PHF carburettors, 40 mm choke. Forced lubrication from 5 kg. oil sump. Electrical system: 12V/ 200W alternator. Battery 12 Ah.
Transmission: primary transmission utilizes gears, secondary transmission utilizes chain drive. Multiple-disc clutch in oil bath. Five-speed gearbox. Kick start.
Frame: duplex cradle (open).
Suspension: at front, telescopic fork; at rear, fork with adjustable shock-absorbers.
Wheels: front and rear 3.50× 18 Racing.
Brakes: front, twin 280 mm discs hydraulically operated, rear, 225 mm disc.
Tank capacity: 4.1 gallons.
Weight: 411 lbs.
Performance: max. speed over 111 mph.

Manufacturer: Ducati Meccanica S.p.A., Via Ducati 3, Bologna

Ducati 500 GTL

Engine: 496.9 cc, twin-cylinder four stroke with parallel cylinders, overhead valve activated by single camshaft and chain drive. Bore and stroke: 78×52 mm. Compression ratio 10:1. Max. power 72 bhp at 9500 rpm. Two Dell'Orto PHF carburettors, 30 mm choke. Electrical system: 12V/150W alternator. 12 Ah battery.

Transmission: primary transmission utilizes gears, secondary transmission utilizes chain drive. Multiple-disc clutch in oil bath. Five-speed gearbox. Electric start.

Frame: open tubular cradle.

Suspension: at front, telescopic fork; at rear, fork with adjustable shock-absorbers.

Wheels: front 3.25×18 rear 3.50×18.

Brakes: front, twin 260 mm discs, rear, 160 mm disc.

Tank capacity: 4.1 gallons.

Weight: 367 lbs.

Performance: max. speed approx. 105 mph.

Manufacturer: Ducati Meccanica S.p.A., Via Ducati 3, Bologna

Ducati 860 GT1

Engine: 864 cc, twin-cylinder arranged longitudinally in 90° V configuration. Four stroke. Single shaft with crown wheel and pinion transmission. Bore and stroke: 86×74.4 mm. Compression ratio: 9.2:1. Max. power not stated. Two Dell' Orto PHF carburettors with 32 mm choke. 12V electrical system. 12Ah battery. Electronic ignition. 220W alternator.

Transmission: primary transmission utilizes gears, secondary transmission utilizes chain drive. Multiple-disc clutch in oil bath. Five-speed gearbox. Kick start (electric start available on request).

Frame: open duplex cradle.

Suspension: at front, telescopic fork; at rear, swinging fork with adjustable shock-absorbers.

Wheels: front, 3.50×18, rear, 4.25×18.

Brakes: front, 280 mm disc (twin disc brake available on request), rear, 210 mm drum.

Tank capacity: 4.1 gallons.

Weight: 462 lbs.

Performance: max. speed approx. 124 mph.

Manufacturer: Ducati Meccanica S.p.A., Via Ducati 3, Bologna

Ducati 900 Desmo SS

Engine: 863.9 cc, twin-cylinder arranged longitudinally in 90° V configuration. Four stroke. Positive timing to overhead valve. Bore and stroke: 86×74.4 mm. Compression ratio: 9.5:1. Max. power not stated. Two Dell'Orto PHM carburettors with 40 mm choke. 12V electrical system. 12 Ah battery. Electronic ignition. 200W alternator.

Transmission: primary transmission utilizes gears, secondary transmission utilizes chain drive. Multiple-disc clutch in oil bath. Five-speed gearbox. Kick start (electric start available on request).

Frame: open tubular frame.

Suspension: at front, telescopic fork; at rear, swinging fork with adjustable shock-absorbers.

Wheels: front, 3.50×18, rear, 3.50×18.

Brakes: front 280 mm disc brake; rear, 225 mm drum.

Tank capacity: 4.1 gallons.

Weight: 413 lbs.

Performance: max. speed approx. 124 mph.

Manufacturer: Ducati Meccanica S.p.A., Via Ducati 3, Bologna

Ducati 860 GTS

Engine: 864 cc, twin-cylinder V transverse 90° four stroke. Bore and stroke: 86×74.4 mm. Compression ratio 9.8:1. Max. power not stated. Twin carburettors Dell'Orto PHF with 32 mm choke. Force feed lubrication with oil sump capacity 5 kg. Electrics 12V. Battery 12 Ah. Electronic ignition. 200W alternator.
Transmission: primary transmission by gears, secondary by chain drive. Multiple-disc clutch in oil bath. Five-speed gearbox. Electric start.
Frame: tubular open cradle.
Suspension: at front, telescopic fork; at rear, swinging fork with adjustable shock-absorber.
Wheels: front 3.50×18, rear 4.00×18.
Brakes: front, 280 mm discs, rear 200 mm drum.
Tank capacity: 3.9 gallons.
Weight: 462 lbs.
Performance. max. speed 124 mph.

Manufacturer: Ducati Meccanica S.p.A., IVa Ducati, 3 Bologna

Fantic Gran Turismo Super

Engine: 49.6 cc, single-cylinder two stroke. Bore and stroke 38.8×42 mm. Compression ratio 12:1. Max. power 8.5 bhp at 10,000 rpm. Dell'Orto SHB 19 carburettor with central float chamber. Electronic ignition.
Transmission: primary transmission utilizes helical, gears, secondary transmission utilizes chain drive. Six-speed gearbox. Kick start.
Frame: duplex cradle.
Suspension: at front, tele-hydraulic fork; at rear, shock-absorbers with non-enclosed springs.
Wheels: front and rear 2.75×18.
Brakes: front hydraulic disc, rear, 118 mm drum.
Tank capacity: 1.7 gallons.
Weight: 171 lbs.
Performance: max. speed 58 mph.

Manufacturer: Fantic Motor, Barzago (Como)

Fantic Caballero 50 RC

Engine: 49.6 cc single-cylinder two stroke producing 9 bhp at 10,000 rpm. Bore and stroke: 38.8×42 mm. Compression ratio 12:1. Dell'Orto VHB 20 BS carburettor. Electronic ignition. High-voltage external coil.
Transmission: primary transmission utilizes helical gears, secondary transmission utilizes chain drive. Six-speed gearbox. Kick start.
Frame: duplex cradle with sump guard.
Suspension: at front, tele-hydraulic fork; at rear, shock-absorbers with enclosed adjustable springs.
Wheels: front 2.50×21, rear 3.50×18.
Brakes: aluminium hubs 124 mm front and rear.
Tank capacity: 1.7 gallons.
Weight: 182 lbs.
Performance: max. speed 49 mph.

Manufacturer: Fantic Motor, Barzago (Como)

Fantic Caballero 50 Regolarità

Engine: 49.6 cc, single-cylinder two stroke producing 6.9 bhp at 11,000 rpm. Bore and stroke, 38.8×42 mm. Compression ratio 11:1. Dell'Orto carburettor SHA 14/12. Ignition: 6V/18W flywheel magneto. High-voltage external coil.
Transmission: primary transmission utilizes helical gears, secondary transmission utilizes chain drive. Four or six-speed gearbox. Kick start.
Frame: duplex cradle with sump guard.
Suspension: at front, tele-hydraulic fork; at rear, shock-absorbers with enclosed springs.
Wheels: front 2.50×19, rear 3.00×17.
Brakes: aluminium hubs 118 mm front and rear.
Tank capacity: 1.7 gallons.
Weight: 151 lbs.
Performance: not stated.

Manufacturer: Fantic Motor, Barzago (Como)

Fantic Caballero 125 CR

Engine: 123.4 cc, single-cylinder two stroke producing 25 bhp at 10,000 rpm. Bore and stroke: 55×52 mm. Compression ratio 12:1. Dell'Orto PHB 32 BS carburettor. Electronic ignition.
Transmission: primary transmission utilizes helical gears, secondary transmission utilizes chain drive. Six-speed gearbox. Kick start.
Frame: duplex cradle.
Suspension: at front, telehydraulic fork; at rear, hydraulic adjustable shock-absorbers.
Wheels: front 3.00×21, rear 4.00×18.
Brakes: 140 mm front, 124 mm rear.
Tank capacity: 1.3 gallons.
Weight: 187 lbs.
Performance: top speed not stated.

Manufacturer: Fantic Motor, Barzago (Como)

Fantic Caballero 125 RC

Engine: 123.48 cc, single-cylinder two stroke producing 21 bhp at 9500 rpm. Bore and stroke: 55×52 mm. Compression ratio 9:1. Dell'Orto PHB 30 carburettor. Ignition: flywheel magneto 6V/33W with high-voltage coil.
Transmission: primary transmission utilizes helical gears, secondary transmission utilizes chain drive. Six-speed gearbox. Kick start.
Frame: duplex cradle.
Suspension: at front, telehydraulic fork; at rear, shock absorbers with adjustable springs.
Wheels: 3.00×21 at the front, 4.00×18 at the rear.
Brakes: aluminium hubs, front 140 mm, rear 124 mm.
Tank capacity: 2.2 gallons.
Weight: 224 lbs.
Performance: max. speed 68 mph.

Manufacturer: Fantic Motor, Barzago (Como)

Fantic Super Rocket

Engine: 49 cc, single-cylinder two stroke producing 4.6 bhp at 9000 rpm. Bore and stroke: 38.8×42 mm. Compression ratio 12:1. Dell'Orto carburettor. Ignition by flywheel magneto 6V/18W. External coil.
Transmission: primary transmission by gears, secondary by chain. Four-speed gearbox. Kick start.
Frame: duplex cradle.
Suspension: at front, telehydraulic fork; at rear, shock-absorbers.
Wheels: front 3.00×12, rear 4.00×10.
Brakes: 180 mm front and rear.
Tank capacity: 1.1 gallons.
Weight: 118 lbs.
Performance: not stated.

Manufacturer: Fantic Motor, Barzago (Como)

Fantic Chopper 125

Engine: 123 cc, single-cylinder two stroke producing 15 bhp at 6800 rpm. Bore and stroke: 55×52 mm. Compression ratio 9:1. VHB 25 Dell'Orto carburettor. Ignition by flywheel magneto 6V/33W with coil.

Transmission: primary transmission by gears, secondary by chain. Five-speed gearbox. Kick start.
Frame: duplex cradle.
Suspension: at front, telehydraulic fork; at rear, shock-absorbers.
Wheels: front 2.75×16, rear 5.00×16.
Brakes: 140 mm front, 123 mm rear.
Tank capacity: 1.75 gallons.
Weight: 228 lbs.
Performance: max. speed 71 mph.

Manufacturer: Fantic Motor, Barzago (Como)

Laverda 250 2TR

Engine: 247 cc, single-cylinder two-stroke with light alloy cylinder. Bore and stroke: 68× 68 mm. Compression ratio 10:1. Max. power 30 bhp at 7000 rpm. Dell'Orto carburettor 32 mm. Electronic Bosch ignition. Battery 12V 6 Ah.

Transmission: primary transmission by gears, secondary by enclosed chain. Multiple-disc dry clutch. Five-speed gearbox. Kick start.

Frame: duplex cradle.

Suspension: at front, telehydraulic fork; at rear, swinging fork with gas shock-absorbers.

Wheels: front 3.00×21, rear 4.00×18.

Brakes: 180 mm front and rear.

Tank capacity: 2.4 gallons.

Weight: 237 lbs.

Performance: max. speed 77 mph.

Manufacturer: Moto Laverda, Breganze, (Vicenza)

Laverda 125

Engine: 124 cc, single-cylinder two-stroke. Bore and stroke: 55× 52 mm. Compression ratio 13.5:1. Max. power not declared. Dell'Orto 32 mm carburettor. Motoplat electronic ignition.

Transmission: primary transmission by gears, secondary by chain drive. Multiple-disc clutch in oil bath. Six-speed gearbox. Kick start.

Frame: tubular single cradle.

Suspension: at front, telescopic fork; at rear, swinging fork.

Wheels: front 3.00×21, rear 4.00×18.

Brakes: drum front and rear.

Tank capacity: 1.7 gallons.

Weight: 180 lbs.

Performance: not stated.

Manufacturer: Moto Laverda, Breganze, (Vicenza)

Laverda 500

Engine: 497 cc, two-cylinder four stroke. Overhead valves driven by camshaft. Bore and stroke: 72×61 mm. Compression ratio and max. power not stated. Twin Dell'Orto PHF 32 mm carburettors. Forced lubrication. Coil contact breaker and automatic advance ignition. Electrics: Bosch 12V, dynamo 150W.

Transmission: primary transmission by triplex chain drive, secondary by chain drive. Six-speed gearbox. Electric start.

Frame: single beam.

Suspension: at front, hydraulic fork; at rear, adjustable shock-absorbers.

Wheels: front, 3.50×18, rear 4.00×18.

Brakes: 280 mm discs front and rear.

Tank capacity: 3.9 gallons.

Weight: 418 lbs.

Performance: max. speed not stated.

Manufacturer: Moto Laverda, Breganze (Vicenza)

Laverda 750 S.F.3

Engine: 743cc, twin-cylinder four stroke producing 65 bhp at 7000 rpm. Overhead valves driven by camshaft. Bore and stroke: 80×74 mm. Compression ratio 9:1. Twin Dell'Orto PHF 36 mm carburettors. Forced lubrication. Ignition: coil, contact breaker and automatic advance. Electrics: Bosch 12V, dynamo 150W. 18 Ah battery.

Transmission: primary transmission by triplex chain drive, secondary by chain drive. Five-speed gearbox. Electric start.

Frame: tubular beam.

Suspension: at front, hydraulic fork, at rear, adjustable hydraulic shock-absorbers.

Wheels: alloy rims front 3.50×18, rear 4.00×18.

Brakes: front 280 mm twin disc, rear 280 mm disc.

Tank capacity: 4.2 gallons.

Weight: 479 lbs.

Performance: max. speed 111 mph.

Manufacturer: Moto Laverda, Breganze (Vicenza)

Laverda 750 GTL Police

Engine: 743 cc, twin-cylinder four stroke. Overhead camshaft. Bore and stroke: 80×74 mm. Compression ratio 8.9:1. Max. power 52 bhp at 6900 rpm. Twin Dell'Orto carburettors 30 mm. Ignition by coil, contact breaker and automatic advance. Electrics: Bosch 12V, dynamo 150W. 18 Ah battery.

Transmission: primary transmission by chain drive, secondary by chain drive. Five-speed gearbox. Electric start.

Frame: tubular with engine integrating the assembly.

Suspension: at front, hydraulic fork; at rear adjustable hydraulic shock-absorbers.

Wheels: front and rear 4.00×18.

Brakes: 230 mm Duplex front and rear.

Tank capacity: 3.7 gallons.

Weight: 528 lbs.

Performance: max. speed approx. 108 mph.

Manufacturer: Moto Laverda, Breganze (Vicenza)

Laverda 1000

Engine: 980 cc, three-cylinder four stroke. Twin overhead camshaft chain driven. Bore and stroke: 75×74 mm. Compression ratio 9:1. Max. power 80 bhp at 7250 rpm. Lubrication by gear pump and radiator for oil cooling. Three Dell'Orto PHF 32 mm carburettors. Electrics: 12V. Bosch 12V electronic ignition. Battery 12V.

Transmission: primary transmission by triple chain drive, secondary by chain drive. Five-speed gearbox. Electric start.

Frame: duplex cradle.

Suspension: at front, telescopic fork; at rear, swinging fork with shock-absorbers.

Wheels: alloy rims front 4.10×18, rear 4.25×18.

Brakes: 280 mm discs front and rear.

Tank capacity: 4.4 gallons.

Weight: 470 lbs.

Performance: max. speed 130 mph.

Manufacturer: Moto Laverda, Breganze (Vicenza)

Moto Guzzi 125 Tuttoterreno

Engine: 120 cc, single-cylinder two stroke producing 15.4 bhp at 7800 rpm. Bore and stroke: 56×49 mm. Compression ratio 9.9:1. Dell'Orto carburettor. Flywheel magneto ignition.

Transmission: primary transmission by gears, secondary transmission by chain drive. Multiple-disc clutch in oil bath. Five-speed gearbox. Kick start.

Frame: duplex cradle.

Suspension: at front, hydraulic fork; at rear, adjustable hydraulic shock-absorbers.

Wheels: front 2.50×21, rear 3.50×18.
Brakes: 135 mm front and rear.

Tank capacity: 1.8 gallons.
Weight: 215 lbs.

Performance: max. speed 68 mph.

Manufacturer: Moto Guzzi S.E.I.M.M., Mandello del Lario (Como)

Moto Guzzi 254

Engine: 231 cc, four-cylinder four-stroke producing 26.6 bhp at 10,500 rpm. Bore and stroke: 44×38 mm. Compression ratio 11.5:1. Ignition: battery and coil. 12V/200W alternator.

Transmission: primary transmission by gears, secondary transmission by semi-enclosed chain drive. Multiple-disc clutch in oil bath. Five-speed gearbox. Electric start.

Frame: tubular.

Suspension: at front, telehydraulic fork; at rear, swinging fork.

Wheels: front 3.00×18, rear 3.25×18.

Brakes: front, hydraulic disc; rear drum.

Tank capacity: 2.5 gallons.

Weight: 257 lbs.

Performance: max. speed 93 mph.

Manufacturer: Moto Guzzi S.E.I.M.M., Mandello del Lario (Como)

Moto Guzzi 250 TS-FD

Engine: 231.4 cc, twin-cylinder two stroke producing 30 bhp at 8000 rpm. Bore and stroke: 56×47 mm. Compression ratio 10:1. Two Dell'Orto VHB 25 BS/BD carburettors. Electronic ignition by means of flywheel and external coils. 6V 9A battery.
Transmission: primary transmission utilizes helical gears, secondary transmission utilizes chain drive. Multiple-disc clutch in oil bath. Five-speed gearbox. Kick start.
Frame: duplex cradle.

Suspension: at front, telescopic fork; at rear, swinging fork.

Wheels: front 3.00×18, rear 3.25×18.

Brakes: front, 260 mm disc, rear 160 mm drum.

Tank capacity: 3.7 gallons.

Weight: 301 lbs.

Performance: max. speed 86 mph.

Manufacturer: Moto Guzzi, S.E.I.M.M., Mandello del Lario (Co)

Moto Guzzi 400 GTS-FD

Manufacturer: Moto Guzzi, S.E.I.M.M., Mandello del Lario (Co)

Engine: 397.2 cc, four-cylinder four stroke, overhead valves activated by camshafts and rocker arms. Bore and stroke: 50×50.6 mm. Compression ratio 10.2:1. Max. power 40 bhp at 9000 rpm. Four Dell'Orto VHB 20 mm carburettors. Ignition by means of battery and induction coil. 12V 15 Ah Bosch alternator.

Transmission: primary transmission utilizes gears. Secondary transmission ulitizes semi-enclosed chain drive. Multiple-disc clutch in oil bath. Five-speed gearbox. Electric/kick start.

Frame: duplex cradle.

Suspension: at front, tele-hydraulic fork; at rear, swinging fork and shock-absorbers.

Wheels: front 3.00×18, rear 3.50×18.

Brakes: front, 300 mm disc, rear, 160 mm drum.

Tank capacity: 3.7 gallons.

Weight: 385 lbs.

Performance: max. speed 105 mph.

Moto Guzzi 850 T3

Manufacturer: Moto Guzzi, S.E.I.M.M., Mandello del Lario (CO)

Engine: 844.05 cc, twin-cylinder four stroke producing 68.5 bhp at 7000 rpm. Overhead valve engine. Bore and stroke 83×78 mm. Compression ratio 9.5:1. Two Dell'Orto VHB 30 C carburettors with 30 mm choke. Forced lubrication of gears employed. Ignition utilizes alternator and induction coil. 14V.-13 Ah electrical system. Battery 32 Ah.

Transmission: primary transmission utilizes helical gears, secondary transmission utilizes prop shaft and universal couplings. Six-speed gearbox. Electric start.

Frame: duplex cradle.

Suspension: at front, hydraulic fork; at rear, swinging fork.

Wheels: front 3.50×18, rear, 4.10×18.

Brakes: integral braking system utilizing dual hydraulic circuits with 300 mm front discs and 242 mm rear disc.

Tank capacity: 5.2 gallons.

Weight: 475 lbs.

Performance: max. speed 120 mph.

Moto Guzzi 850 T3 California

Engine: 844.05 cc, twin-cylinder four stroke producing 68.5 bhp at 7000 rpm. Overhead valve engine. Bore and stroke 83×78 mm. Compression ratio 9.5:1. Two Dell'Orto VHB 29 C carburettors with 30 mm choke. Forced lubrication of gears employed. Ignition utilizes alternator and induction coil. Electrical system 14V.-13 Ah.

Transmission: primary transmission utilizes helical gears, secondary transmission utilizes prop shaft with universal couplings. Five-speed gearbox. Electric start.

Frame: duplex cradle.

Suspension: at front, hydraulic fork; at rear, swinging fork.

Wheels: front and rear 4.00 ×18.

Brakes: integral braking system utilizing dual hydraulic circuits which act upon 2 300 mm front discs and 1 242 mm rear disc.

Tank capacity: 5.2 gallons.

Weight: 495 lbs.

Performance: max. speed 117 mph.

Manufacturer: Moto Guzzi, S.E.I.M.M., Mandello del Lario (CO)

Moto Guzzi 850 'Le Mans'

Engine: 844 cc, twin-cylinder four stroke. Overhead valve. Bore and stroke: 83×78 mm. Compression ratio: 10.2:1. Max. power 81 bhp at 7600 rpm. Carburettors with 36 mm choke. Ignition system utilizes double contact breakers, double condensers, double high voltage coils. Electrical system: 14V with 14V alternator. 13 Amp. Battery 32 Ah.

Transmission: primary transmission utilizes helical gears, secondary transmission utilizes prop shaft and universal couplings. Five-speed gearbox. Electric start.

Frame: duplex cradle.

Suspension: at front, telehydraulic fork; at rear, swinging fork.

Wheels: front 3.50×18, rear 4.10×18.

Brakes: front, twin 300 mm discs, rear, 242 mm disc.

Tank capacity: 4.9 gallons.

Weight: 435 lbs.

Performance: max. speed 130 mph.

Manufacturer: Moto Guzzi, S.E.I.M.M., Mandello del Lario (Co)

Moto Guzzi V 1000 Convert

Engine: 949 cc, twin-cylinder four stroke producing 71 bhp at 6500 rpm. Overhead valve. Bore and stroke: 88×78 mm. Compression ratio: 9.2:1. Two carburettors. Battery ignition with twin contact breakers. 12V/350W electrical system.

Transmission: primary transmission utilizes gears, secondary transmission utilizes prop shaft and universal couplings. Gear change by means of two speed hydraulic torque convertor. Electric start.

Frame: duplex cradle.

Suspension: telescopic with hydraulic shock-absorbers.

Wheels: front and rear 4.10 ×18.

Brakes: hydraulically operated twin disc front brake and single disc rear brake. Foot control for rear brake and left front brake; manual control for right front brake.

Tank capacity: 5.5 gallons.

Weight: 528 lbs.

Performance: max. speed: lower gear ratio 83 mph; high gear ratio 105 mph.

Manufacturer: Moto Guzzi, S.E.I.M.M., Mandello del Lario (Co)

Moto Morini 125

Engine: 122.96 cc, single-cylinder four stroke, valve gear with push rods and rocker arms, flat head with parallel valves. Bore and stroke: 59×45 mm. Compression ratio 11.7:1. Max. power 15.3 SAE bhp at 9000 rpm. VHB 24 BS carburettor, central, with 24 mm choke. Electronic ignition—electronic contact breaker. 6V 9Ah electrical system.

Transmission: primary transmission utilizes gears with helical teeth, secondary transmission utilizes semi-enclosed chain drive. Multiple-disc clutch in oil bath. Six-speed gearbox. Foot-operated. Kick start.

Frame: duplex cradle.

Suspension: at front, telehydraulic fork; at rear, swinging fork.

Wheels: front 2.75×18, rear 3.00×18.

Brakes: front 260 mm disc, rear 136 mm drum.

Tank capacity: 2.6 gallons.

Weight: 235 lbs.

Performance: max. speed approx. 77 mph.

Manufacturer: Moto Morini, Via A. Bergami, 7, Bologna

Moto Morini Super Scrambler 50

Engine: 48.82 cc, single-cylinder four stroke. Bore and stroke: 41×37 mm. Max. power not stated. 14 mm diameter carburettor. Forced lubrication. Ignition by means of external coil. 6V/18W electrical system with alternator.

Transmission: primary transmission utilizes helical gears, secondary transmission utilizes chain drive. Four-speed gearbox. Kick start.

Frame: duplex cradle.

Suspension: at front, telescopic fork; at rear, swinging fork.

Wheels: front and rear 2.50×17.

Brakes: 104 mm front and rear.

Tank capacity: 1.5 gallons.

Weight: 123 lbs.

Performance: not stated.

Manufacturer: Moto Morini, Via A. Bergami, 7, Bologna

Moto Morini $3\frac{1}{2}$ Strada

Engine: 344 cc, twin-cylinder four stroke engine in V longitudinal configuration. Heads and cylinders of light alloy. Bore and stroke 62×57 mm. Compression ratio 10:1. Max. power 35 bhp at 8200 rpm. Two Dell'Orto VHB 25 BS carburettors. Forced lubrication at gears. Electronic ignition. Electrical system with 12V 9Ah battery.

Transmission: primary transmission utilizes gears, secondary transmission utilizes chain drive. Six-speed gearbox. Kick start.

Frame: duplex cradle.

Suspension: at front, hydraulic fork; at rear, adjustable hydraulic shock-absorbers.

Wheels: front 3.25×18, rear 4.10×18.

Brakes: front 200 mm, rear 160 mm.

Tank capacity: 3 gallons.

Weight: 316 lbs.

Performance: max. speed 102 mph.

Manufacturer: Moto Morini, Via A. Bergami, 7 Bologna

Moto Morini $3\frac{1}{2}$ Sport

Engine: 344 cc, twin-cylinder four stroke in V longitudinal configuration. Heads and cylinders of light alloy. Bore and stroke: 62×57 mm. Compression ratio 11:1. Max. power 39 bhp DIN at 8500 rpm. Two Dell'Orto VHB 25 BS carburettors. Forced lubrication at gears. Electronic ignition. Electrical system: 12V 9Ah battery.

Transmission: primary transmission utilizes gears, secondary transmission utilizes chain drive. Six-speed gearbox. Kick start.

Frame: duplex cradle.

Suspension: at front, tele-hydraulic fork; at rear, adjustable tele-hydraulic shock-absorbers.

Wheels: front 3.25×18, rear 4.10×18.

Brakes: front 260 mm disc, rear 180 mm drum.

Tank capacity: 3 gallons.

Weight: 316 lbs.

Performance: max. speed 108 mph.

Manufacturer: Moto Morini, Via A. Bergami, 7, Bologna

SWM Silver Vase ES 125 (ER 125)

Engine: 123 cc, single-cylinder two stroke, light alloy cylinder. Bore and stroke: 54×54 mm. Compression ratio 13.5:1 (13:1). Max. power 24 (23) bhp at 9500 (9200) rpm. Concentric carburettor with 32 mm choke. Ignition by Motoplat Thyristor 6V/35W.

Transmission: primary transmission by gears, secondary by semi-enclosed chain. Seven-speed gearbox. Kick start.

Frame: duplex cradle.
Suspension: at front, telehydraulic fork; at rear, swinging fork with shock-absorbers.

Wheels: front 3.00×21, rear 4.00×18.
Brakes: 140 mm front and rear.

Tank capacity: 1.9 gallons.
Weight: 209 lbs.

Performance: not stated.

Manufacturer: SWM, Via Pascoli 7, 20030 Palazolo Milanese

SWM Cross 125 'Replica'

Engine: 123 cc, single-cylinder two stroke light alloy cylinder. Bore and stroke: 54×54 mm. Compression ratio 14:1. Max. power 24 bhp at 11,500 rpm. Carburettor with 32 mm choke. Motoplat electronic ignition 6V/35W.

Transmission: primary transmission by gears, secondary by semi-enclosed chain. Multiple-disc clutch in oil bath. Five-speed gearbox. Kick start.

Frame: duplex cradle.
Suspension: at front, telehydraulic fork; at rear, swinging fork with shock-absorbers.

Wheels: front 3.00×21, rear 4.00×18.
Brakes: 140 mm front and rear.

Tank capacity: 1.75 gallons.

Weight: 182 lbs.

Performance: not stated.

Manufacturer: SWM, Via Pascoli 7, 20030 Palazolo Milanese

SWM Silver Vase ES 250 (ES 175)

Engine: 248 (173) cc, single-cylinder, two stroke. Bore and stroke: 71×61 (60×61) mm. Compression ratio 10:1 (11.5:1). Max. power 34 bhp at 7500 (28 at 8800) rpm. 36 mm (34 mm) choke. Ignition by 6V/35W Motoplat flywheel magneto.

Transmission: primary transmission by gears, secondary by semi-enclosed chain. Multiple-disc clutch in oil bath. Seven-speed gearbox. Kick start.

Frame: duplex cradle.

Suspension: at front, telehydraulic fork; at rear, swinging fork with shock-absorbers.

Wheels: front 3.00×21, rear 4.50×18.

Brakes: 140 mm front and rear.

Tank capacity: 2 gallons.

Weight: 220 lbs (213).

Performance: not stated.

Manufacturer: SWM, Via Pascoli 7, 20030 Palazolo Milanese

Vespa 125 Primavera ET3

Engine: 121 cc, single-cylinder two stroke. Bore and stroke: 51×55 mm. Compression ratio and max power not stated. Electronic ignition.

Transmission: primary transmission by gears, secondary by chains. Multiple-disc clutch in oil bath. Four-speed gearbox.

Frame: pressed-steel fabrication.

Suspension: pivoted-link front and rear.
Wheels: 3.00×10 front and rear.
Brakes: drum brakes front and rear.

Tank capacity: 1.8 gallons.

Weight: 171 lbs.

Performance: max. speed 57 mph.

Manufacturer: Piaggio & C., Via A. Cecchi 6, Genova

Vespa 200 Rally

Engine: 197 cc, single-cylinder two stroke producing 12 bhp at 5700 rpm. Compression ratio 8:1. Bore and stroke: 66.5×57 mm. Dell'Orto carburettor. Electronic ignition 6V/50W.
Transmission: primary transmission by gears, secondary by chain. Multiple-disc clutch in oil bath. Four-speed gearbox. Kick start.

Frame: pressed-steel fabrication.

Suspension: helical springs. Hydraulic shock-absorbers.

Wheels: 3.50×10 front and rear.

Brakes: drum brakes front and rear.

Tank capacity: 1.8 gallons.

Weight: 235 lbs.

Performance: 68 mph.

Manufacturer: Piaggio & C., Via A. Cecchi 6, Genova

Vespa 125 TS

Engine: 123 cc, single-cylinder two stroke. Bore and stroke: 52.5×57 mm. Max. power and compression ratio not stated. Dell'Orto carburettor. Ignition by flywheel magneto 6V/50W.

Transmission: primary transmission by gears, secondary by chain. Multiple-disc clutch in oil bath. Four-speed gearbox. Kick start.

Frame: pressed-steel fabrication.

Suspension: helical springs. Hydraulic shock-absorbers.

Wheels: 3.50×10 front and rear.

Brakes: drum brakes front and rear.

Tank capacity: 1.8 gallons.

Weight: 222 lbs.

Performance: max. speed 57 mph.

Manufacturer: Piaggio & C., Via Cecchi 6, Genova

Honda 125 IAP

Engine: 122 cc, single-cylinder four-stroke, light alloy cylinder. Bore and stroke: 56×49.5 mm. Compression ratio 9.5:1. Max. power 10 bhp at 8000 rpm. 22 mm Keihin carburettor. 6V fly-wheel magneto ignition.
Transmission: primary transmission by gears, secondary by non-enclosed chain drive. Multiple-disc clutch in oil bath. Five-speed gearbox. Kick start.
Frame: tubular beam.
Suspension: at front, telehydraulic fork; at rear, swinging fork.
Wheels: front 2.75×21, rear 3.25×18.
Brakes: front disc, rear drum.
Tank capacity: 2.2 gallons.
Weight: 242 lbs.
Performance: max. speed 74 mph.

Manufacturer: Honda Motor Co. Ltd, Tokyo

Honda CB 200

Engine: 198 cc, twin-cylinder four stroke of light alloy. Bore and stroke: 55.5×41 mm. Max. power 17 bhp at 9000 rpm. Compression ratio 9:1. Twin Keihin carburettors with centre float chamber. Ignition: coil and battery. Alternator 12V/110W.
Transmission: primary transmission by gears, secondary by non-enclosed chain drive. Multiple-disc clutch in oil bath. Five-speed gearbox. Electric start.
Frame: duplex cradle.
Suspension: at front, telehydraulic fork; at rear, swinging fork.
Wheels: front 2.75×18, rear 3.00×18.
Brakes: front disc, rear drum.
Tank capacity: 2 gallons.
Weight: 292 lbs.
Performance: max. speed 80 mph.

Manufacturer: Honda Motor Co. Ltd, Tokyo

Honda XL 125

Engine: 124 cc, single cylinder four stroke producing 12.5 bhp at 10,000 rpm. Bore and stroke 56×49 mm. Compression ratio 9.3:1. Keihin 22 mm carburettor. Ignition by battery and coil.
Transmission: primary transmission by gears, secondary by chain. Multiple-disc clutch in oil bath. Five-speed gearbox. Kick start.
Frame: single tubular strut.
Suspension: at front, telehydraulic fork; at rear, swinging fork.
Wheels: front 2.75×21, rear, 4.00×18.
Brakes: front 130 mm, rear 120 mm.
Tank capacity: 1.5 gallons.
Weight: 222 lbs.
Performance: max. speed 65 mph.

Manufacturer: Honda Motor Co. Ltd, Tokyo

Honda XL 250

Engine: 248 cc, single-cylinder four stroke producing 20 bhp at 8000 rpm. Bore and stroke: 74×57.8 mm. Compression ratio 9.1:1. Keihin 28 mm carburettor. Ignition by battery and coil. 6V/80W alternator.
Transmission: primary transmission by gears, secondary by chain. Multiple-disc clutch in oil bath. Five-speed gearbox. Kick start.
Frame: semi-double cradle.
Suspension: at front, telehydraulic fork; at rear, swinging fork.
Wheels: front 2.75×21, rear 4.00×18.
Brakes: 150 mm at front, 140 mm at rear.
Tank capacity: 1.7 gallons.
Weight: 299 lbs.
Performance: max. speed 77 mph.

Manufacturer: Honda Motor Co. Ltd, Tokyo

Honda CB 250 G

Engine: 249 cc, twin-cylinder four stroke (Twin) producing 27 bhp at 9500 rpm. Single camshaft operated valve gear. Bore and stroke: 56×50.6 mm. Compression ratio 9.5:1. Two Keihin 32 mm vacuum carburettors. Forced lubrication. Ignition by means of battery and induction coil. 12V/130W alternator.
Transmission: primary transmission utilizes gears, secondary transmission utilizes semi-enclosed chain drive. Multiple-disc clutch in oil bath. Six-speed gearbox. Electric start.
Frame: duplex cradle.
Suspension: at front, tele-hydraulic fork; at rear, swinging fork.
Wheels: front 3.00×18, rear 3.50×18.
Brakes: front 260 mm, rear 160 mm.
Tank capacity: 2.4 gallons.
Weight: 363 lbs.
Performance: max. speed 88 mph.

Manufacturer: Honda Motor Co. Ltd, Tokyo

Honda CB 360 G

Engine: 356 cc, twin-cylinder four stroke. Bore and stroke: 67×50.6 mm Compression ratio: 9.3:1. Max. power 34 bhp at 9000 rpm. Two 32 mm Keihin carburettors. Ignition by means of battery and induction coil with alternator.
Transmission: primary transmission utilizes gears, secondary transmission utilizes non-enclosed chain drive. Multiple-disc clutch in oil bath. Six-speed gearbox. Electric/Kick start.
Frame: duplex cradle.
Suspension: at front, tele-hydraulic fork; at rear, swinging fork.
Wheels: front 3.00×18, rear 3.50×18.
Brakes: front, 260 mm disc, rear, 160 mm drum.
Tank capacity: 2.4 gallons.
Weight: 366 lbs.
Performance: max. speed 99 mph.

Manufacturer: Honda Motor Co. Ltd, Tokyo

Honda CB 400 F

Engine: 408 cc, four-cylinder four stroke driven by a single overhead camshaft. Bore and stroke: 51×50 mm. Compression ratio 9.4:1. Max. power 37 bhp at 8500 rpm. Four Keihin carburettors with 20 mm central float chamber. Ignition by means of battery and ignition coil. 12V/150W alternator.

Transmission: primary transmission utilizes toothed chain drive, secondary transmission utilizes semi-enclosed chain drive. Multiple-disc clutch in oil bath. Six-speed gearbox. Electric/Kick start.

Frame: duplex cradle.

Suspension: at front, tele-hydraulic fork; at rear, swinging fork.

Wheels: front 3.00×18, rear 3.50×18.

Brakes: front, discs, rear, drum.

Tank capacity: 3.1 gallons.

Weight: 375 lbs.

Performance: max. speed 105 mph.

Manufacturer: Honda Motor Co. Ltd, Tokyo

Honda CB 500 Four

Engine: 498 cc, four-cylinder four stroke driven by a single overhead camshaft. Bore and stroke: 56×50.6 mm. Compression ratio 9:1. Max. power 50 bhp at 9000 rpm. Four Keihin 22 mm carburettors. Ignition by means of battery and induction coil. 12V/200W alternator.
Transmission: primary transmission utilizes toothed chain drive, secondary transmission utilizes semi-enclosed chain drive. Multiple-disc clutch in oil bath. Five-speed gearbox. Electric/Kick start.
Frame: duplex cradle.
Suspension: at front, telehydraulic fork; at rear, swinging fork.
Wheels: front 3.25×19, rear 3.50×18.
Brakes: front hydraulic disc, rear drum.
Tank capacity: 3 gallons.
Weight: 421 lbs.
Performance: max. speed 108 mph.

Manufacturer: Honda Motor Co. Ltd, Tokyo

Honda CB 500 T

Engine: 498 cc, twin-cylinder four stroke with parallel cylinders. Bore and stroke: 70×64.8 mm. Compression ratio 9:1. Max. power 42 bhp at 8000 rpm. Two Keihin carburettors, 36 mm vacuum. Forced lubrication. Ignition by means of battery and induction coil, 12V 130W alternator.
Transmission: primary transmission utilizes gears, secondary transmission utilizes semi-enclosed chain drive. Multiple-disc clutch in oil bath. Five-speed gearbox. Electric/Kick start.
Frame: duplex cradle.
Suspension: at front, telehydraulic fork; at rear, swinging fork.
Wheels: front, 3.25×19, rear, 3.75×18.
Brakes: front disc hydraulically operated, rear 180 mm drum.
Tank capacity: 3.3 gallons.
Weight: 462 lbs.
Performance: max. speed 105 mph.

Manufacturer: Honda Motor Co. Ltd, Tokyo

Honda CB 550 Super Sport

Engine: 539 cc, four-cylinder four stroke. Bore and stroke: 58.5×50.6 mm. Compression ratio 9:1. Max. power 50 bhp at 8500 rpm. Four Keihin 22 mm carburettors. Ignition by means of battery and induction coil. 12V/200W alternator.

Transmission: primary transmission utilizes toothed chain drive, secondary transmission utilizes semi-enclosed chain drive. Multiple-disc clutch in oil bath. Five-speed gearbox. Electric start.

Frame: duplex cradle.

Suspension: at front, telehydraulic fork; at rear, swinging fork.

Wheels: front 3.25×19, rear 3.75×18.

Brakes: front 280 mm disc, rear, 180 mm drum.

Tank capacity: 3.7 gallons.

Weight: 453 lbs.

Performance: max. speed 111 mph.

Manufacturer: Honda Motor Co. Ltd, Tokyo

Honda CB 750 Super Sport

Engine: 736 cc, four-cylinder four stroke in line engine. Bore and stroke: 61 × 63 mm. Compression ratio 9.2:1. Max. power 67 nhp at 8000 rpm. Four Keihin carburettors with 28 mm choke. Ignition by means of battery and induction coil. 12V/210W alternator.

Transmission: primary transmission utilizes chain drive, secondary transmission utilizes chain drive. Multiple-disc clutch in oil bath. Five-speed gearbox. Electric/Kick start.

Frame: duplex cradle.

Suspension: at front, tele-hydraulic fork; at rear, swinging fork with shock-absorbers.

Wheels: front 3.25 × 19, rear, 4.00 × 18.

Brakes: front and rear, 296 mm discs.

Tank capacity: 3.7 gallons.

Weight: 480 lbs.

Performance: max. speed 124 mph.

Manufacturer: Honda Motor Co. Ltd, Tokyo

Honda GL 1000 Gold Wing

Engine: 999 cc, four-cylinder four stroke, horizontally opposed cylinders. Bore and stroke: 72 × 51.4 mm. Compression ratio 9:1. Max. power: 80 bhp at 7900 rpm. 4 Keihin carburettors. Forced lubrication. 12V/280W battery alternator.
Transmission: primary transmission utilizes chain drive, secondary transmission utilizes prop shaft and universal couplings. Multiple-disc clutch in oil bath. Five-speed gearbox. Electric start.
Frame: duplex cradle.
Suspension: at front, telescopic fork; at rear, swinging fork.
Wheels: front, 3.50 × 19, rear, 4.50 × 17.
Brakes: front twin disc, rear single disc.
Tank capacity: 3.9 gallons.
Weight: 569 lbs.
Performance: 124 mph max. speed.

Manufacturer: Honda Motor Co. Ltd, Tokyo

Kawasaki 100 G4 TR

Engine: 99 cc, single cylinder two stroke producing 11 bhp at 7500 rpm. Bore and stroke: 49.5 × 51.8. Compression ratio: 7:1. 19 mm Mikuni carburettor. Flywheel magneto ignition.
Transmission: primary by gears, secondary by chain semi-enclosed. Multiple disc clutch in oil bath. Five-speed gearbox. Kick start.
Frame: duplex cradle.
Suspension: at front, tele-hydraulic fork; at rear, swinging fork.
Wheels: front 2.50 × 18, rear 2.75 × 18.
Brakes: 110 mm front and rear.
Tank capacity: 2.2 gallons.
Weight: 196 lbs.
Performance: max speed 69 mph.

Manufacturer: Kawasaki Heavy Industries Ltd., Motorcycle Division, World Trade Center Building, Tokyo

Kawasaki KH 100

Engine: 99 cc, single-cylinder two-stroke producing 11.5 bhp at 8000 rpm. Bore and stroke: 49.5×51.8 mm. Compression ratio 7:1. 6V fly-wheel magneto ignition.

Transmission: primary transmission by gears, secondary by chain. Multiple-disc clutch in oil bath. Five-speed gearbox. Kick start.

Frame: duplex cradle.
Suspension: at front, telehydraulic fork, at rear, swinging fork.

Wheels: front 3.00×18, rear 2.75×18.

Brakes: 130 mm front and rear.

Tank capacity: 2.2 gallons.

Weight: 196 lbs.

Performance: max. speed 71 mph.

Manufacturer: Kawasaki Heavy Industries Ltd, Motorcycle Division, World Trade Center Building, Tokyo

Kawasaki KE 125

Engine: 124 cc, single-cylinder two stroke producing 13 bhp at 6500 rpm. Bore and stroke: 56×50.6 mm. Compression ratio 6.5:1. Forced lubrication. Ignition: flywheel magneto, external coil, 6V. Raised exhaust pipe.

Transmission: primary transmission utilizes gears, secondary transmission utilizes nonenclosed chain drive. Multiple-disc clutch in oil bath. Six-speed gearbox. Kick start.
Frame: duplex cradle.

Suspension: at front, telehydraulic fork; at rear, swinging fork.

Wheels: front 2.75×21, rear 3.50×18.

Brakes: 120 mm front and rear.

Tank capacity: 1.6 gallons.

Weight: 218 lbs.

Performance: max. speed 68 mph.

Manufacturer: Kawasaki Heavy Industries Ltd, Motorcycle Division, World Trade Center Building, Tokyo

Kawasaki KX 125

Engine: 124 cc, single-cylinder two stroke. Bore and stroke: 56×56.5 mm. Compression ratio 8:1. Max. power 22 bhp at 9750 rpm. Mikuni 26 mm carburettor. Independent lubrication using pump operation. Flywheel magneto ignition.

Transmission: primary transmission utilizes gears, secondary transmission utilizes semi-enclosed chain drive. Multiple-disc clutch in oil bath. Six-speed gearbox. Kick start.

Frame: duplex cradle.
Suspension: at front, telehydraulic fork; at rear, swinging fork.

Wheels: front 3.00×21, rear, 4.10×18.
Brakes: 120 mm front and rear.

Tank capacity: 1.4 gallons.

Weight: 178 lbs.

Performance: not stated.

Manufacturer: Kawasaki Heavy Industries Ltd, Motorcycle Division, World Trade Center Building, Tokyo

Kawasaki KH 250

Engine: 249 cc, three-cylinder two stroke transversely mounted. Bore and stroke: 45 × 52.5 mm. Compression ratio 7.5:1. Max. power 28 bhp at 7500 rpm. Three 22 mm Mikuni carburettors. Ignition by battery and coil.
Transmission: primary transmission by gears, secondary by chain. Multiple-disc clutch in oil bath. Five-speed gearbox. Kick start.
Frame: duplex cradle.
Suspension: at front, telehydraulic fork; at rear, swinging fork.
Wheels: front 3.25 × 18, rear 3.50 × 18.
Brakes: front 226 mm, rear 180 mm.
Tank capacity: 3 gallons.
Weight: 353 lbs.
Performance: 90 mph.

Manufacturer: Kawasaki Heavy Industries Ltd, Motorcycle Division, World Trade Center Building, Tokyo

Kawasaki KX 250

Engine: 246 cc, single-cylinder two stroke. Bore and stroke: 69.5×64.9 mm. Compression ratio 7.9:1. Max. power 34 bhp at 8000 rpm. Forced lubrication. Thyristor contactless ignition. Raised exhaust pipe.
Transmission: primary transmission utilizes gears, secondary transmission utilizes non-enclosed chain drive. Multiple-disc clutch in oil bath. Five-speed gearbox. Kick start.
Frame: duplex cradle.
Suspension: at front, telehydraulic fork; at rear, swinging fork.
Wheels: front 3.00×21, rear 4.60×18.
Brakes: 130 mm front and rear.
Tank capacity: 2 gallons.
Weight: 198 lbs.
Performance: not stated.

Manufacturer: Kawasaki Heavy Industries Ltd, Motorcycle Division, World Trade Center Building, Tokyo

Kawasaki Z 400

Engine: 398 cc, twin-cylinder four stroke producing 35 bhp at 9000 rpm. Bore and stroke: 64×62 mm. Compression ratio 9.4:1. 2 keihin 36 mm carburettors. Battery/induction coil ignition. Electrical system: 12V alternator. Lubrication using a separate pump.

Transmission: primary transmission utilizes gears, secondary transmission utilizes chain drive. Multiple-disc clutch in oil bath. Five-speed gearbox. Electric/Kick start.

Frame: duplex cradle.

Suspension: at front, telehydraulic fork; at rear, swinging fork.

Wheels: front 3.25×18, rear 3.50×18.

Brakes: front, 226 mm discs, rear, 180 mm drum.

Tank capacity: 3 gallons.

Weight: 386 lbs.

Performance: max. speed 99 mph approx.

Manufacturer: Kawasaki Heavy Industries Ltd, Motorcycle Division, World Trade Center Building, Tokyo

Kawasaki KH 400

Engine: 400 cc, three-cylinder, two stroke. Bore and stroke: 57×52.3 mm. Compression ratio 6.5:1. Max. power 42 bhp at 7000 rpm. 3 Mikuni carburettors. Electronic Thyristor contactless ignition.
Transmission: primary transmission utilizes gears, secondary transmission utilizes chain drive. Multiple-disc clutch in oil bath. Five-speed gearbox. Kick start.
Frame: duplex cradle.
Suspension: at front, telehydraulic fork; at rear, swinging fork.
Wheels: front 3.25×18, rear 3.50×18.
Brakes: front, 226 mm disc, rear, 180 mm drum.
Tank capacity: 3 gallons.
Weight: 364 lbs.
Performance: max. speed approx. 105 mph.

Manufacturer: Kawasaki Heavy Industries Ltd, Motorcycle Division, World Trade Center Building, Tokyo

Kawasaki KH 500

Engine: 498 cc, three-cylinder two-stroke producing 59 bhp at 8000 rpm. Bore and stroke: 60×58.5 mm. Compression ratio 6.8:1. Three 28 mm Mikuni carburettors. 12V alternator.
Transmission: primary transmission by gears, secondary by chain. Multiple-disc clutch in oil bath. Five-speed gearbox. Kick start.
Frame: duplex cradle.
Suspension: at front, telehydraulic fork; at rear, swinging fork.
Wheels: front 3.25×19, rear 4.00×18.
Brakes: 245 mm disc at front, 180 mm at rear.
Tank capacity: 3.5 gallons.
Weight: 428 lbs.
Performance: max. speed approx. 124 mph.

Manufacturer: Kawasaki Heavy Industries Ltd, Motorcycle Division, World Trade Center Building, Tokyo

Kawasaki Z 750

Engine: 745 cc, twin-cylinder four stroke. Bore and stroke: 78×78 mm. Compression ratio 8.5:1. Max. power 55 bhp at 7000 rpm. 2 Mikuni 38 mm carburettors. Battery-induction coil ignition. Electrical system, 12V alternator. Forced lubrication.

Transmission: primary transmission utilizes gears, secondary transmission utilizes chain drive. Multiple-disc clutch in oil bath. Five-speed gearbox. Electric/Kick start.

Frame: duplex cradle.

Suspension: at front, telehydraulic fork; at rear, swinging fork.

Wheels: front 3.25×19, rear 4.00×18.

Brakes: front 226 mm disc, rear 180 mm drum.

Tank capacity: 3.1 gallons.

Weight: 479 lbs.

Performance: max. speed 111 mph approx.

Manufacturer: Kawasaki Heavy Industries Ltd, Motorcycle Division, World Trade Center Building, Tokyo

Kawasaki Z 900

Engine: 903 cc, four-cylinder four stroke, overhead valve driven by double overhead cam-shafts. Bore and stroke: 66×66 mm. Compression ratio 8.5:1. Max. power 82 bhp at 8500 rpm. Four Mikuni carburettors, 24 mm in diameter. Battery-induction coil ignition, 12V alternator.

Transmission: primary transmission utilizes gears, secondary transmission utilizes semi-enclosed chain drive. Multiple-disc clutch in oil bath. Five-speed gearbox. Electric/Kick start.

Frame: duplex cradle.

Suspension: at front, telescopic fork; at rear, swinging fork with adjustable shock-absorbers.

Wheels: front 3.25×19, rear 4.00×18.

Brakes: front, 245 mm discs; rear, 200 mm brake.

Tank capacity: 3.9 gallons.

Weight: 531 lbs.

Performance: max. speed 124 mph.

Manufacturer: Kawasaki Heavy Industries Ltd, Motorcycle Division, World Trade Center Building, Tokyo.

Suzuki TS 400

Engine: 396 cc, single-cylinder two-stroke, light alloy cylinder. Bore and stroke: 82×75 mm. Compression ratio 6.5:1. Max. power 34 bhp at 6000 rpm. Mikuni concentric carburettor 32 mm. Ignition: fly-wheel magneto. Pump lubrication.
Transmission: primary transmission by gears, secondary by open chain. Multiple-disc clutch in oil bath. Five-speed gearbox. Kick start.
Frame: duplex cradle.
Suspension: at front, telescopic fork; at rear, swinging fork.
Wheels: front 3.00×21, rear 4.00×18.
Brakes: 150 mm front and rear.
Tank capacity: 1.8 gallons.
Weight: 253 lbs.
Performance: max. speed 84 mph.

Manufacturer: Suzuki Motor Co. Ltd, P.O. Box 116, Hamamatsu 430

Suzuki 500 Sport TT

Engine: 492 cc, twin-cylinder two stroke producing 44 bhp at 6000 rpm. Bore and stroke: 70×64 mm. Compression ratio 6.6:1. Twin carburettors with 32 mm choke. Alternator 12V 8A.
Transmission: primary transmission by gears, secondary by chain drive. Multiple-disc clutch in oil bath. Five-speed gearbox. Kick start.
Frame: duplex cradle.
Suspension: at front, telehydraulic fork; at rear, swinging fork with adjustable shock-absorbers.
Wheels: front 3.25×19, rear 4.00×18.
Brakes: front 200 mm, rear 180 mm.
Tank capacity: 3.7 gallons.
Weight: 363 lbs.
Performance: max. speed 114 mph.

Manufacturer: Suzuki Motor Co. Ltd, P.O. Box 116, Hamamatsu 430

Suzuki GT 380

Engine: 371 cc, three-cylinder two stroke, air cooled. Bore and stroke: 54×54 mm. Compression ratio 7.0:1. Max. power 37 bhp at 7500 rpm. Three Mikuni carburettors with 24 mm choke. Pressure pump lubrication. Ignition: battery and coil. Alternator 12V/200W.

Transmission: primary transmission by gears, secondary by semi-enclosed chain drive. Multiple-disc clutch in oil bath. Six-speed gearbox. Kick start.

Frame: duplex cradle.

Suspension: at front, telescopic fork; at rear, swinging fork with adjustable shock-absorber.

Wheels: front 3.00×19, rear 3.50×18.

Brakes: front 295 mm disc, rear 180 mm drum.

Tank capacity: 3.3 gallons.

Weight: 377 lbs.

Performance: max. speed 104/108 mph.

Manufacturer: Suzuki Motor Co. Ltd, P.O. Box 116 Hamamatsu 430

Suzuki GT 500

Engine: 492 cc, twin-cylinder two-stroke (Twin). Bore and stroke: 70×64 mm. Compression ratio 6.6:1. Max. power 44 bhp at 6000 rpm. Two carburettors with 32 mm choke. Ignition by means of battery and induction coil. 12V 8A alternator.
Transmission: primary transmission utilizes gears, secondary transmission utilizes semi-enclosed chain drive. Multiple-disc clutch in oil bath. Five-speed gearbox. Kick start.
Frame: duplex cradle.
Suspension: at front, tele-hydraulic fork; at rear, swinging fork with adjustable shock-absorbers.
Wheels: front 3.25×19, rear, 4.00×18.
Brakes: front disc, rear 180 mm drum.
Tank capacity: 3.7 gallons.
Weight: 395 lbs.
Performance: max. speed approx. 104/109 mph.

Manufacturer: Suzuki Motor Co. Ltd, P.O. Box 116, Hamamatsu 430

Suzuki GT 550

Engine: 543 cc, three-cylinder two-stroke. Bore and stroke: 61×62 mm. Compression ratio 6.8:1. Max. power 53 bhp at 7500 rpm. Three carburettors with 28 mm choke. Forced lubrication. Ignition by means of battery and induction coil. 12V/210W alternator.
Transmission: primary transmission utilizes gears, secondary transmission utilizes chain drive. Multiple-disc clutch in oil bath. Five-speed gearbox. Electric start.
Frame: duplex cradle.
Suspension: at front, tele-hydraulic fork; at rear, swinging fork.
Wheels: front 3.25×19, rear 4.00×18.
Brakes: front 275 mm disc, rear, 180 mm drum.
Tank capacity: 3.3 gallons.
Weight: 441 lbs.
Performance: max. speed approx. 114/119 mph.

Manufacturer: Suzuki Motor Co. Ltd, P.O. Box 116, Hamamatsu 430

Suzuki Rotary RE-5

Engine: 497 cc, internal combustion NSU Wankel single rotor engine, water-cooled with automatic fan. Max. power 62 bhp at 6500 rpm. One 18-32 HHD Solex low pressure carburettor. Forced lubrication. Ignition by means of 12V battery and induction coil. Bifurcating exhaust pipe.

Transmission: primary transmission utilizes duplex chain drive, secondary transmission utilizes enclosed chain drive. Multiple-disc clutch in oil bath. Five-speed gearbox. Electric start.

Frame: duplex cradle.

Suspension: at front, telescopic fork; at rear, swinging fork.

Wheels: front 3.50×19, rear 4.00×18.

Brakes: front 298 mm twin discs, rear 181 mm drum.

Tank capacity: 3.7 gallons.

Weight: 550 lbs.

Performance: max. speed 110/114 mph.

Manufacturer: Suzuki Motor Co. Ltd, P.O. Box 116, Hamamatsu 430

Suzuki GT 750

Engine: 738 cc, three-cylinder two stroke, water-cooled with forced circulation and thermostatic control. It also has a fan so that cooling is effected in neutral. Bore and stroke: 70×64 mm. Compression ratio 6.9:1. Max. power 70 bhp at 6500 rpm. Three Mikuni carburettors with 40 mm choke. Forced lubrication. Ignition by means of battery and induction coil with three circuit breakers. 12V 280W alternator.

Transmission: primary transmission utilizes gears, secondary transmission utilizes semi-enclosed chain drive. Multiple-disc clutch in oil bath. Five-speed gearbox. Electric start.

Frame: duplex cradle.

Suspension: at front, telescopic fork; at rear, swinging fork with adjustable shock-absorbers.

Wheels: front 3.25×19, rear, 4.00×18.
Brakes: front, 295 mm twin discs, rear, Duplex 180 mm drums.

Tank capacity: 3.7 gallons.
Weight: 506 lbs.

Performance: max. speed 119/124 mph.

Manufacturer: Suzuki Motor Co. Ltd, P.O. Box 116, Hamamatsu 430

Yamaha RD 50

Engine: 49 cc, single cylinder two stroke producing 6.2 bhp at 8250 rpm. Bore and stroke: 40 × 39.7 mm. Compression ratio 6.4:1. Mikuni carburettor with 20 mm choke. Flywheel magneto ignition 6V/35W.
Transmission: primary by gears, secondary by semi-enclosed chain. Multiple-disc clutch in oil bath. Five-speed gearbox. Kick start.

Frame: duplex cradle.

Suspension: at front, tele-hydraulic fork, at rear, swinging fork.

Wheels: front 2.50×17, rear 2.75×17.
Brakes: front disc, rear 110 mm drum.

Tank capacity: 1.75 gallons.
Weight: 167 lbs.

Performance: max. speed 52 mph.

Manufacturer: Yamaha Motor Co. Ltd., 1280 Nakajo, Hamakita-Shi, Shizuoka-Ken

Yamaha FS 50

Engine: 49 cc, single cylinder two stroke producing 5 bph at 8500 rpm. Bore and stroke: 40× 39.7 mm. Compression ratio 6.8:1. 16 mm Mikuni carburettor. 6V flywheel magneto ignition.

Transmission: primary by gears, secondary by semi-enclosed chain. Multiple-disc clutch in oil bath. Five-speed gearbox. Kick start.

Frame: not stated.

Suspension: at front, tele-hydraulic fork; at rear, swinging fork.

Wheels: front 2.50×17, rear 2.75×17.
Brakes: 110 mm front and rear.

Tank capacity: 1.5 gallons.

Weight: 189 lbs.

Performance: max. speed 52 mph.

Manufacturer: Yamaha Motor Co. Ltd., 1280 Nakajo, Hamakita-Shi, Shizuoka-Ken

Yamaha RS 100

Engine: 97 cc, single-cylinder two stroke producing 10.3 bhp at 7500 rpm. Bore and stroke: 52×45.6 mm. Compression ratio 6.7:1. 20 mm Mikuni carburettor. Ignition by flywheel magneto 6V 35/18W.

Transmission: primary transmission by gears, secondary by chain. Five-speed gearbox. Kick start.

Frame: duplex cradle.
Suspension: at front, tele-hydraulic fork; at rear, swinging fork.

Wheels: front 2.75 × 18, rear 2.75×18.

Brakes: 110 mm drum brakes front and rear.

Tank capacity: 2 gallons.

Weight: 213 lbs.

Performance: max. speed 68 mph.

Manufacturer: Yamaha Motor Co. Ltd, 1280 Nakajo, Hamakita-Shi, Shizuoka-Ken

Yamaha RD 125

Engine: 124 cc, twin-cylinder two stroke. Bore and stroke: 43×43 mm. Compression ratio 6.8:1. Max. power 16 bhp at 9500 rpm. Two Teikei carburettors with 18 mm choke. Ignition by means of battery and induction coil.
Transmission: primary by gears, secondary by semi-enclosed chain drive. Multiple-disc clutch in oil bath. Foot-operated gear change. Five-speed gearbox. Electric start.
Frame: duplex cradle.
Suspension: at front, telescopic fork; at rear, swinging fork.
Wheels: front 2.50×18, rear, 2.75×18.
Brakes: front 150 mm disc, rear 130 mm drum.
Tank capacity: 2.5 gallons.
Weight: 233 lbs.
Performance: max. speed 77 mph.

Manufacturer: Yamaha Motor Co. Ltd, 1280 Nakajo, Hamakita-Shi Shizuoka-Ken

Yamaha RD 200

Engine: 195 cc, twin-cylinder two stroke. Bore and stroke 52×46 mm. Compression ratio 7.1:1. Max. power 22 bhp at 7500 rpm. Teikei 20 mm carburettor. Forced lubrication. Ignition by means of battery and induction coil.
Transmission: primary transmission utilizes gears, secondary transmission utilizes non-enclosed chain drive. Multiple-disc clutch in oil bath. Five-speed gearbox. Electric start.
Frame: duplex cradle.
Suspension: at front, tele-hydraulic fork; at rear, swinging fork.
Wheels: front 2.75×18, rear 3.00×18.
Brakes: front 180 mm, rear 150 mm.
Tank capacity: 2.5 gallons.
Weight: 255 lbs.
Performance: max. speed 83 mph.

Manufacturer: Yamaha Motor Co. Ltd, 1280 Nakajo, Hamakita-Shi Shizuoka-Ken

Yamaha RD 250

Engine: 247 cc, twin-cylinder two-stroke "torque induction" engine. Bore and stroke: 54×54 mm. Compression ratio 6.7:1. Max. power 30 bhp at 7500 rpm. 2 Mikuni carburettors, 28 mm choke. Ignition by means of battery and induction coil. 12V alternator.

Transmission: primary transmission utilizes gears, secondary transmission utilizes enclosed chain drive. Multiple-disc clutch in oil bath. Five-speed gearbox. Kick start.

Frame: duplex cradle.

Suspension: at front, tele-hydraulic fork; at rear, swinging fork.

Wheels: front 3.00×18, rear 3.25×18.

Brakes: front 267 mm disc, rear 180 mm.

Tank capacity: 3.5 gallons.

Weight: 308 lbs.

Performance: max. speed 93 mph.

Manufacturer: Yamaha Motor Co. Ltd, 1280 Nakajo, Hamakita-Shi Shizuoka-Ken

Yamaha YZ 250

Engine: 246 cc, single-cylinder two-stroke producing 34 bhp at 8000 rpm. Bore and stroke: 70×64 mm. Compression ratio 7.8:1. 34 mm Mikuni carburettor Thyristor flywheel magneto ignition.
Transmission: primary transmission by gears, secondary by chain. Multiple-disc clutch in oil bath. Five-speed gearbox. Kick start.
Frame: duplex cradle.
Suspension: at front, telehydraulic fork; at rear, swinging fork.
Wheels: front 3.00×21, rear 4.60×18.
Brakes: 160 mm front, 130 mm rear.
Tank capacity: 1.5 gallons.
Weight: 213 lbs.
Performance: max. speed not stated.

Manufacturer: Yamaha Motor Co. Ltd, 1280 Nakajo, Hamakita-Shi, Shizuoka-Ken

Yamaha TY 250

Engine: 246 cc, single-cylinder two-stroke producing 16 bhp at 6000 rpm. Bore and stroke: 70×64 mm. Compression ratio 6.2:1. 26 mm Mikuni carburettor.

Transmission: primary transmission by gears, secondary by chain. Multiple-disc clutch in oil bath. Five-speed gearbox. Kick start.
Frame: duplex cradle.
Suspension: at front telehydraulic fork; at rear, swinging fork.
Wheels: front 3.00×21, rear 4.60×18.
Brakes: 130 mm front, 110 mm rear.
Tank capacity: 1.3 gallons.
Weight: 233 lbs.
Performance: max. speed not stated.

Manufacturer: Yamaha Motor Co. Ltd, 1280 Nakajo, Hamakita-Shi, Shizuoka-Ken

Yamaha RD 400

Engine: 398 cc, twin-cylinder two stroke. Bore and stroke: 64×62 mm. Compression ratio 6.2:1. Max. power: 40 bhp at 7500 rpm. Two concentric carburettor. Battery ignition.

Transmission: primary transmission utilizes gears, secondary transmission utilizes semi-enclosed chain drive. Six-speed gearbox. Kick start.

Frame: duplex cradle.

Suspension: at front, telehydraulic fork, at rear, swinging fork with shock-absorbers.

Wheels: front, 3.00×18, rear, 3.50×18.

Brakes: front 260 mm disc, rear drum.

Tank capacity: 3.6 gallons.

Weight: 345 lbs.

Performance: 102 mph.

Manufacturer: Yamaha Motor Co. Ltd, 1280 Nakajo, Hamakita-Shi Shizuoka-Ken

Yamaha DT 400

Engine: 397 cc single-cylinder two stroke producing 20 bhp at 5500 rpm. Bore and stroke: 85×70 mm. Compression ratio 6.4:1. Mikuni carburettor with 28 mm choke. Forced lubrication. Ignition by means of battery and induction coil. Mitsubishi 12V/100W alternator.
Transmission: primary transmission utilizes gears, secondary transmission utilizes non-enclosed chain drive. Multiple-disc clutch in oil bath. Five-speed gearbox. Kick start.
Frame: duplex cradle.
Suspension: at front, telescopic fork; at rear swinging fork.
Wheels: front 3.00×21, rear 4.00×18.
Brakes: front and rear, conical brakes.
Tank capacity: 1.9 gallons.
Weight: 275 lbs.
Performance: max. speed not stated.

Manufacturer: Yamaha Motor Co. Ltd, 1280 Nakajo, Hamakita-Shi Shizuoka-Ken

Yamaha XS 500

Engine: 498 cc, twin-cylinder four stroke (Twin). Four valves per cylinder actuated by camshaft. Bore and stroke: 73×59.6 mm. Compression ratio 8.5:1. Max. power 49 bhp at 8500 rpm. Two carburettors with 32 mm choke. Ignition by means of battery and induction coil. 12V alternator.
Transmission: primary transmission utilizes gears, secondary transmission utilizes non-enclosed chain drive. Multiple-disc clutch in oil bath. Five-speed gearbox. Electric start.
Frame: duplex cradle.
Suspension: at front, telescopic fork; at rear, swinging fork.
Wheels: front 3.25×19, rear, 4.00×18.
Brakes: front and rear, disc brakes.
Tank capacity: 3.3 gallons.
Weight: 424 lbs.
Performance: max. speed 111 mph.

Manufacturer: Yamaha Motor Co. Ltd, 1280 Nakajo, Hamakita-Shi Shizuoka-Ken

Yamaha 500 XT

Engine: 499 cc, single-cylinder four-stroke producing 28.2 bhp at 5400 rpm. Bore and stroke: 87×84 mm. Compression ratio 9:1. Mikuni carburettor 38 mm. Fly-wheel magneto ignition.

Transmission: primary transmission by chain drive, secondary by semi-enclosed chain drive. Multiple-disc clutch in oil bath. Five-speed gearbox. Kick start.

Frame: tubular cradle.

Suspension: at front, tele-hydraulic fork; at rear, swinging fork with shock-absorbers.

Wheels: front 3.00×21, rear 4.00×18.

Brakes: 180 mm front and rear.

Tank capacity: 2.2 gallons.

Weight: 303 lbs.

Performance: not stated.

Manufacturer: Yamaha Motor Co. Ltd, 1280 Nakajo, Hamakita-Shi Shizuoka-Ken

Yamaha XS 650

Engine: 653 cc, twin-cylinder four stroke (Twin) OHC. Bore and stroke: 75×74 mm. Compression ratio 8.4:1. Max. power 50.1 bhp at 7200 rpm. Two Mikuni carburettors. Ignition by means of battery and induction coil. 12V alternator.

Transmission: primary transmission utilizes gears, secondary transmission utilizes enclosed chain drive. Multiple-disc clutch in oil bath. Five-speed gearbox. Electric/Kick start.

Frame: duplex cradle.

Suspension: at front, telehydraulic fork; at rear, swinging fork.

Wheels: front 3.25×19, rear, 4.00×18.

Brakes: front, twin 298 mm discs, rear, 180 mm brake.

Tank capacity: 3.3 gallons.

Weight: 473 lbs.

Performance: max. speed 114 mph.

Manufacturer: Yamaha Motor Co. Ltd, 1280 Nakajo, Hamakita-Shi Shizuoka-Ken

Yamaha 750 Z

Engine: 747 cc, three-cylinder four-stroke, twin overhead camshafts with lateral drive. Bore and stroke: 68×68.6 mm. Compression ratio not given. Max. power not stated. 3 Mikuni 34 mm vacuum carburettors. Contact breaker ignition with 10 mm sparking plug.

Transmission: primary transmission utilizes gears, secondary transmission utilizes universal couplings on the left side. Multiple-disc clutch in oil bath. Five-speed gearbox. Electric start.

Frame: duplex cradle.

Suspension: at front, telehydraulic fork; at rear, swinging fork with shock-absorbers.

Wheels: light alloy rims, front, 3.50×19, rear, 4.00×18.

Brakes: 298 mm discs front and rear.

Tank capacity: 4 gallons.

Weight: not stated.

Performance: not stated.

Manufacturer: Yamaha Motor Co. Ltd, 1280 Nakajo, Hamakita-Shi Shizuoka-Ken

Bultaco Lobito T 74/125

Engine: 124.9 (174.7) cc, single-cylinder two stroke. Bore and stroke: 51.5×60 (60.9×60) mm. Compression ratio 10:1. Max. power 11.2 bhp at 7000 rpm (16.6 bhp at 5500 rpm). Amal 25 mm carburettor. Flywheel magneto ignition with battery.
Transmission: primary transmission utilizes gears, secondary transmission utilizes chain drive. Multiple-disc clutch in oil bath. Five-speed gearbox. Kick start.
Frame: duplex cradle.
Suspension: at front, telescopic fork; at rear, swinging fork.
Wheels: front 3.00×19, rear 3.50×18.
Brakes: front, 140 mm, rear, 125 mm.
Tank capacity: 1.2 gallons.
Weight: 194 lbs.
Performance: not stated.

Manufacturer: Bultaco – Compañia Española de Motores, S.A., Barcelona

Bultaco Metralla GT 250

Engine: 244 cc, single-cylinder two stroke. Bore and stroke: 72×60 mm. Compression ratio 9:1. Max. power 27.6 bhp at 7500 rpm. Amal 32 mm carburettor. Femsa 6V/40W flywheel magneto ignition.
Transmission: primary transmission utilizes chain drive, secondary transmission utilizes enclosed chain drive. Multiple-disc clutch in oil bath. Five-speed gearbox. Kick start.
Frame: single tubular beam.
Suspension: at front, telehydraulic fork; at rear, swinging fork.
Wheels: front 2.75×18, rear 3.00×18.
Brakes: 160 mm front and rear.
Tank capacity: 3 gallons.
Weight: 224 lbs.
Performance: max. speed not stated.

Manufacturer: Bultaco – Compañia Española de Motores, S.A., Barcelona

Bultaco Pursang 200

Engine: 196 cc, single-cylinder two stroke. Bore and stroke: 64×60 mm. Compression ratio 13:1 (12–11). Max. power 24.5 bhp at 7000 rpm. Flywheel magneto ignition.
Transmission: primary transmission utilizes gears, secondary transmission utilizes non-enclosed chain drive. Multiple-disc clutch in oil bath. Five-speed gearbox. Kick start.
Frame: duplex cradle.
Suspension: at front, telescopic fork; at rear, swinging fork.
Wheels: front 3.00×21, rear 4.00×18.
Brakes: front, 140 mm, rear, 125 mm.
Tank capacity: 1.5 gallons.
Weight: 209 lbs.
Performance: not stated.

Manufacturer: Bultaco – Compañia Española de Motores, S.A. Barcelona

Bultaco Sherpa T 250

Engine: 244 cc, single-cylinder two stroke producing 14.4 bhp at 5500 rpm. Bore and stroke: 72×60 mm. Compression ratio 9:1. Amal concentric 27 mm carburettor. Flywheel magneto 6V/40W ignition with external coil.
Transmission: primary transmission utilizes chain drive, secondary transmission utilizes semi-enclosed chain drive. Five-speed gearbox. Kick start.
Frame: duplex cradle.
Suspension: at front, telehydraulic fork; at rear, swinging fork with shock-absorbers.
Wheels: front 2.75×21, rear 4.00×18.
Brakes: front, 140 mm, rear, 125 mm.
Tank capacity: 0.9 gallons.
Weight: 199 lbs.
Performance: max. speed not

Manufacturer: Bultaco – Compañia Española de Motores, S.A., Barcelona

Bultaco Frontera 250/370

Engine: 244.3 cc (363.16), single-cylinder two stroke with light alloy cylinders. Bore and stroke: 72×60 (85×64) mm. Compression ratio 12:1 (10.5:1). Max. power 32 bhp at 8000, (33 at 7000) rpm. Amal 20 (36) mm carburettor. Electrical system, flywheel magneto, alternator.

Transmission: primary transmission utilizes duplex chain drive, secondary transmission utilizes open chain drive. Five-speed gearbox. Kick start.

Frame: duplex cradle.

Suspension: at front, tele-hydraulic fork; at rear, swinging fork with adjustable shock-absorbers.

Wheels: front 3.00×21, rear 4.00×18.

Brakes: 140 mm front and rear.

Tank capacity: 2.5 gallons.

Weight: 231 lbs.

Performance: not stated.

Manufacturer: Bultaco – Compañia Española de Motores, S.A., Barcelona

Bultaco Alpina 250/350

Engine: 244 cc, single-cylinder two-stroke. Bore and stroke: 72×60 mm. Compression ratio 9:1. Mas. power 17.5 bhp at 5500 rpm. Amal concentric 27 mm carburettor. Fly-wheel magneto ignition with outside coil 6V 35W.

Transmission: primary transmission by Duplex chain, secondary by non-enclosed chain drive. Multiple-disc clutch in oil bath. Five-speed gearbox. Kick start.
Frame: duplex cradle.
Suspension: at front, tele-hydraulic fork; at rear, swinging fork with shock-absorbers.
Wheels: front 3.00×21, rear 4.00×18.
Brakes: 140 mm front and rear.
Tank capacity: 2.3 gallons.
Weight: 215 lbs.
Performance: not stated.

Manufacturer: Bultaco, Compañia Española de Motores, S.A., Barcelona

Bultaco Matador Mk9 350

Engine: 326 cc, single-cylinder two-stroke. Bore and stroke: 83.2×60 mm. Compression ratio 9:1. Max. power 17.5 bhp at 5500 rpm. Amal concentric 27 mm carburettor. Flywheel magneto ignition with external coil 6V/40W.
Transmission: primary transmission by chain, secondary by semi-enclosed chain. Multiple-disc clutch in oil bath. Five-speed gearbox. Kick start.
Frame: duplex cradle.
Suspension: at front, tele-hydraulic fork; at rear, swinging fork with shock-absorbers.
Wheels: front 2.75×21; rear 4.00×18.
Brakes: front 140 mm, rear 125 mm.
Tank capacity: 1 gallon.
Weight: 200 lbs.
Performance: max. speed not stated.

Manufacturer: Bultaco, Compañia Española de Motores, S.A., Barcelona

Derbi Grand Prix SL

Engine: 187 cc, twin-cylinder two stroke producing 26 bhp at 8000 rpm. Bore and stroke: 51.5×45 mm. Compression ratio 10:1. Twin-choke carburettor 22-24 mm. 12V 45/21W flywheel magneto ignition.

Transmission: primary transmission by gears, secondary by chain. Multiple-disc clutch in oil bath. Six-speed gearbox. Kick start.

Frame: duplex cradle.

Suspension: at front, telehydraulic fork; at rear, swinging fork with shock-absorbers.

Wheels: front 2.75×18, rear 3.00×18.

Brakes: front double discs, rear 170 mm drum.

Tank capacity: 3 gallons.

Weight: 275 lbs.

Performance: not stated.

Manufacturer: Nacional Motor S.A. Derbi, Barcelona/ Mollet

Montesa Rapita 50

Engine: 48.75 cc, single-cylinder two stroke. Bore and stroke: 38×43 mm. Compression ratio 9:1. Max. power not stated. Dell'Orto SHA 14-14 mm carburettor. Motoplat flywheel ignition with external coil.

Transmission: primary transmission utilizes gears, secondary transmission utilizes semi-enclosed chain drive. Multiple-disc clutch in oil bath. Three-speed gearbox. Kick start.
Frame: single beam.
Suspension: at front, telescopic fork; at rear, swinging fork.
Wheels: front 2.25×19, rear 3.00×18.
Brakes: 110 mm front and rear.
Tank capacity: 1.3 gallons.
Weight: 121 lbs.
Performance: max. speed 24 mph.

Manufacturer: Permanyer S.A. de Industrias Mecanicas, Avenida de la Electricidad, Esplugas, Barcelona

Montesa Cappra 125 VA

Engine: 123 cc, single-cylinder two stroke. Bore and stroke: 54×54mm. Compression ratio 14:1. Max. power not stated. Bing Concentric 32 mm carburettor. Contactless ignition.
Transmission: primary transmission utilizes gears, secondary transmission utilizes chain drive. Multiple disc clutch in oil bath. Six-speed gearbox. Kick start.
Frame: single cradle.
Suspension: at front, telescopic fork; at rear, swinging fork.
Wheels: front 3.00×21, rear 4.00×18.
Brakes: 130 mm front and rear.
Tank capacity: 1.3 gallons.
Weight: 195 lbs.
Performance: not stated.

Manufacturer: Permanyer S.A. de Industrias Mecanicas, Avenida de la Electricidad, Esplugas, Barcelona

Montesa Cota 123

Engine: 123 cc, single-cylinder two stroke. Bore and stroke: 38×43 mm. Compression ratio 9:1. 25 mm Amal carburettor. Motoplat ignition. Max. power not stated. Raised exhaust.

Transmission: primary transmission by gears, secondary by chain. Multiple-disc clutch in oil bath. Six-speed gearbox. Kick start.

Frame: duplex cradle.
Suspension: at front, telehydraulic fork; at rear, swinging fork.

Wheels: front, 2.50×20, rear 3.75×17.

Brakes: 110 mm front and rear.

Tank capacity: 1 gallon.

Weight: 156 lbs.

Performance: max. speed 43 mph.

Manufacturer: Permanyer S.A. de Industrias Mecanicas, Avenida de la Electricidad, Esplugas, Barcelona

Montesa Cota 172

Engine: 157 cc, single-cylinder two stroke. Bore and stroke: 60.9×54 mm. Compression ratio 11:1. Max. power not stated. 20 mm Amal carburettor. Raised exhaust.

Transmission: primary transmission by gears, secondary by chain. Multiple-disc clutch in oil bath. Six-speed gearbox. Kick start.

Frame: duplex cradle.
Suspension: at front, telehydraulic fork; at rear, swinging fork.

Wheels: front 2.50×20, rear 3.75×17.

Brakes: 110 mm front and rear.

Tank capacity: 1 gallon.

Weight: 171 lbs.

Performance: max. speed 65-68 mph.

Manufacturer: Permanyer S.A. de Industrias Mecanicas, Avenida de la Electricidad, Esplugas, Barcelona

Montesa Cota 247 'Ulf Karlson'

Engine: 247.7 cc, single-cylinder two stroke. Bore and stroke: 72.5×60 mm. Compression ratio 10:1. Max. power not stated. Amal concentric 27 mm carburettor. Raised exhaust pipe.

Transmission: primary transmission utilizes gears, secondary transmission utilizes nonenclosed chain drive. Multiple-disc clutch in oil bath. Five-speed gearbox. Kick start.

Frame: single beam.
Suspension: at front, telehydraulic fork, at rear, swinging fork.

Wheels: front 2.75×21, rear 4.00×18.

Brakes: 110 mm, front and rear.

Tank capacity: 1.2 gallons.

Weight: 191 lbs.

Performance: max. speed 65 mph.

Manufacturer: Permanyer S.A. de Industrias Mecanicas, Avenida de la Electricidad, Esplugas, Barcelona

Montesa 250 King Scorpion/Automix

Engine: 246.3 cc, single-cylinder two stroke. Bore and stroke: 70×64 mm. Compression ratio 12:1. Max. power not stated. Bing concentric 32 mm carburettor. Oil injection. Thyristor ignition.
Transmission: primary transmission utilizes gears, secondary transmission utilizes non-enclosed chain drive. Multiple-disc clutch in oil bath. Five-speed gearbox. Kick start.
Frame: duplex cradle.
Suspension: at front, tele-hydraulic fork; at rear, swinging fork.
Wheels: front 2.75×21, rear 4.00×18.
Brakes: front 150 mm, rear 130 mm.
Tank capacity: 2.2 gallons.
Weight: 242 lbs.
Performance: max. speed 86 mph.

Manufacturer: Permanyer S.A. de Industrias Mecanicas, Avenida de la Electricidad, Esplugas, Barcelona

Mototrans-Ducati 50 Mini 3

Engine: 47.6 cc, single-cylinder two stroke. Bore and stroke: 42×38. Compression ratio 9.5:1. Max. power 2.3 bhp at 5200 rpm. SHA 14-14 mm carburettor. Flywheel magneto ignition with battery.
Transmission: primary transmission utilizes helical gears. Secondary transmission utilizes chain drive. Multiple-disc clutch in oil bath. Three-speed gearbox. Kick start.
Frame: duplex cradle.
Suspension: at front, telescopic fork; at rear, swinging fork.
Wheels: front and rear 00× 12.
Brakes: 100 mm drum, front and rear.
Tank capacity: 1.1 gallons.
Weight: 123 lbs.
Performance: max speed 24 mph.

Manufacturer: Maquinaria y Elementos De Transporte S.A. (Mototrans) Almogalvares 181, Barcelona

Mototrans-Ducati 350 Vento

Engine: 340.2 cc, single-cylinder four stroke. Bore and stroke: 76×75 mm. Compression ratio 9.5:1. Max. power 28 bhp at 7500 rpm. Amal 30 mm carburettor. Overhead valve gear. Battery lighting, recharged by means of a flywheel alternator. Electronic adjustment of current. 6V/60W electrical system.

Transmission: primary transmission utilizes gears, secondary transmission utilizes semi-enclosed chain drive. Multiple-disc clutch in oil bath. Five-speed gearbox. Kick start.

Frame: tubular steel.

Suspension: at front, tele-hydraulic fork; at rear, swinging fork with shock-absorbers.

Wheels: front 3.25×18, rear 4.00×18.

Brakes: front, 230 mm discs, rear, 200 mm drum.

Tank capacity: 3.5 gallons.

Weight: 286 lbs.

Performance: max. speed 99 mph.

Manufacturer: Maquinara y Elementos De Transporte S.A. (Mototrans), Almogalvares 181, Barcelona.

Ossa 125 Enduro Phantom

Engine: 125 cc, single-cylinder two stroke. Bore and stroke: 54×54 mm. Compression ratio 9:1. Max. power not stated. Concentric Bing 36 mm carburettor. Thyristor Motoplat ignition. 6W alternator.
Transmission: primary transmission utilizes duplex chain drive, secondary transmission utilizes semi-enclosed chain drive. Multiple-disc clutch in oil bath. Five-speed gearbox. Kick start.
Frame: duplex cradle.
Suspension: at front, tele-hydraulic fork; at rear, swinging fork with shock-absorbers.
Wheels: front 3.00×21, rear 4.00×18.
Brakes: 122 mm rear, 150 mm front.
Tank capacity: 2 gallons.
Weight: 204 lbs.
Performance: max. speed 71 mph.

Manufacturer: Maquinaria Cinematografica S.A., (Ossa Motorcycles), Poligno Industrial Zona Franca, Barcelona

Ossa 250 Explorer

Engine: 250 cc, single-cylinder two stroke. Bore and stroke: 72×60 mm. Compression ratio 9:1. Max. power not stated. Concentric Bing 27 mm carburettor. Thyristor Motoplat contactless ignition. 6W alternator.
Transmission: primary transmission utilizes duplex chain drive, secondary transmission utilizes semi-enclosed chain drive. Multiple-disc clutch in oil bath. Five-speed gearbox. Kick start.
Frame: duplex cradle.
Suspension: at front, tele-hydraulic fork; at rear, swinging fork with shock-absorbers.
Wheels: front 3.00×21, rear 4.00×18.
Brakes: 122 mm front and rear.
Tank capacity: 2 gallons.
Weight: 194 lbs.
Performance: max. speed 74 mph.

Manufacturer: Maquinaria Cinematografica S.A., (Ossa Motorcycles), Poligno Industrial Zona Franca, Barcelona

Ossa 250 Tourist

Engine: 250 cc, single-cylinder two stroke. Light alloy cylinder. Bore and stroke: 60×72 mm. Compression ratio 12:1. Max. power not stated. Amal carburettor with 32 mm choke. Motoplat flywheel magneto ignition. 6V/8A battery.

Transmission: primary transmission utilizes gears, secondary transmission utilizes semi-enclosed chain drive. Multiple-disc clutch in oil bath. Five-speed gearbox. Kick start.

Frame: duplex cradle.

Suspension: at front, tele-hydraulic fork; at rear, swinging fork.

Wheels: front 3.00×19, rear 3.25×18.

Brakes: 163 mm front and rear.

Tank capacity: 2.9 gallons.

Weight: 235 lbs.

Performance: max. speed 86 mph.

Manufacturer: Maquinaria Cinematografica S.A., (Ossa Motorcycles), Poligno Industrial Zona Franca, Barcelona

Ossa 250 Super Pioneer

Engine: 250 cc, single-cylinder two stroke. Bore and stroke: 72×60 mm. Compression ratio 9:1. Max. power not stated. 32 mm Amal carburettor. Motoplat Thyristor ignition. 6W alternator.
Transmission: primary transmission by chain, secondary by chain. Multiple-disc clutch in oil bath. Five-speed gearbox. Kick start.
Frame: duplex cradle.
Suspension: at front, telehydraulic fork; at rear, swinging fork.
Wheels: front 3.00×21, rear 4.00×18.
Brakes: front 150 mm, rear 122 mm.
Tank capacity: 2.8 gallons.
Weight: 214 lbs.
Performance: max. speed 80 mph.

Manufacturer: Maquinaria Cinematografica S.A., (Ossa Motocycles), Poligno Industrial Zona Franca, Barcelona

Ossa 250 Trial

Engine: 250 cc, single-cylinder two stroke. Bore and stroke: 72×60 mm. Compression ratio 9:1. 27 mm Amal Carburettor. Motoplat Thyristor ignition. Max. power not stated. 6W alternator.
Transmission: primary transmission by chain, secondary by chain. Multiple-disc clutch in oil bath. Five-speed gearbox. Kick start.
Frame: duplex cradle.
Suspension: at front, telehydraulic fork; at rear, swinging fork.
Wheels: front 2.75×21, rear 4.00×18.
Brakes: 122 mm drum brakes front and rear.
Tank capacity: 1.3 gallons.
Weight: 191 lbs.
Performance: not stated.

Manufacturer: Maquinaria Cinematografica S.A., (Osso Motorcycles), Poligno Industrial Zona Franca, Barcelona

Ossa 350 MAR

Engine: 350 cc, single-cylinder two stroke. Bore and stroke: 77×65 mm. Compression ratio 9:1. Max. power not stated. Amal concentric 27 mm carburettor. Thyristor Motoplat ignition. 6W alternator.
Transmission: primary transmission utilizes duplex chain drive, secondary transmission utilizes non-enclosed chain drive. Multiple-disc clutch in oil bath. Four-speed gearbox. Kick start.
Frame: duplex cradle.
Suspension: at front, telehydraulic fork; at rear, swinging fork with shock-absorbers.
Wheels: front 2.75×21, rear 4.00×18.
Brakes: 122 mm front and rear.
Tank capacity: 1.3 gallons.
Weight: 191 lbs.
Performance: max. speed 74 mph.

Manufacturer: Maquinaria Cinematografica S.A., (Ossa Motorcycles), Poligno Industrial Zona Franca, Barcelona

Ossa 350 Enduro

Engine: 350 cc, single-cylinder two stroke. Bore and stroke: 77×65 mm. Compression ratio 9:1. Max. power not stated. Amal concentric 32 mm carburettor. Thyristor Motoplat contactless ignition. 6W alternator.
Transmission: primary transmission utilizes duplex chain drive, secondary transmission utilizes non-enclosed chain drive. Multiple-disc clutch in oil bath. Four-speed gearbox. Kick start.
Frame: duplex cradle.
Suspension: at front, telehydraulic fork; at rear, swinging fork with shock-absorbers.
Wheels: front 3.00×21, rear 4.50×18.
Brakes: 163 mm front and rear.
Tank capacity: 2.8 gallons.
Weight: 211 lbs.
Performance: max. speed 83 mph.

Manufacturer: Maquinaria Cinematografica S.A., (Ossa Motorcycles), Poligno Industrial Zona Franca, Barcelona

Sanglas 400 E

Engine: 423 cc, single-cylinder four-stroke, vertical cylinder. Bore and stroke: 82.5×79 mm. Compression ratio 8:1. Max. power 30 bhp at 6500 rpm. Amal concentric 30 mm carburettor. Ignition: battery and coil 12V/110W Femsa.

Transmission: primary transmission by duplex chain secondary transmission by chain. Multiple-disc clutch in oil bath. Four-speed gearbox. Electric start.

Frame: duplex cradle.

Suspension: at front, tele-hydraulic fork; at rear, swinging fork with shock-absorbers.

Wheels: front 3.25×18; rear 4.00×18.

Brakes: 180 mm front and rear.

Tank capacity: 3.3 gallons.

Weight: 369 lbs.

Performance: max. speed 99 mph.

Manufacturer: Sanglas, S.A. Rambla Justo Oliveras, S.N. Hospitalet, Barcelona

Husqvarna Automatic 360

Engine: 354 cc, single-cylinder two stroke. Light alloy cylinder with chromium-plated linings. Bore and stroke: 82×67 mm. Compression ratio 10.5:1. Max. power not stated. Bing carburettor with 36 mm choke. Contactless Motoplat-Thyristor ignition, CDI, 6V/35W.

Transmission: primary transmission utilizes gears, secondary transmission utilizes non-enclosed chain drive. Multiple-disc clutch in oil bath. Four-speed automatic gearbox.

Frame: tubular single beam.

Suspension: at front, Husqvarna tele-hydraulic fork; at rear, swinging fork with shock-absorbers.

Wheels: front 3.00×21, rear 4.75×18.

Brakes: front 140 mm; rear 160 mm.

Tank capacity: 2.5 gallons.

Weight: 215 lbs.

Performance: not stated.

Manufacturer: Husqvarna Vapenfabriks, AB, Huskvarna

Husqvarna MC 125 CR-76

Engine: 124 cc, single-cylinder two stroke, light alloy wide finned cylinder. Bore and stroke: 55×52 mm. Compression ratio 13.5:1. Max. power not stated. Bing carburettor with 32 mm choke, Motoplat CDI ignition. **Transmission:** primary transmission utilizes gears, secondary transmission utilizes totally-enclosed chain drive. Multiple-disc clutch in oil bath. Six-speed gearbox. **Frame:** single tubular beam. **Suspension:** at front, tele-hydraulic fork; at rear, swinging fork. **Wheels:** front 3.00×21, rear 4.00×18. **Brakes:** 120 mm front & rear. **Tank capacity:** 1.7 gallons. **Weight:** 196 lbs. **Performance:** max. speed not stated.

Manufacturer: Husqvarna Vapenfabriks, AB, Huskvarna

Husqvarna MC 360 CR-76

Engine: 354 cc, single-cylinder two stroke. Bore and stroke 69.5×64.5 mm. Compression ratio: 12.3:1. Max. power not stated. Bing Carburettor with 36 mm choke. Forced lubrication. Motoplat Thyristor ignition. **Transmission:** primary transmission utilizes gears, secondary transmission utilizes chain drive. Multiple-disc clutch in oil bath. Six-speed gearbox. Kick start. **Frame:** tubular single beam. **Suspension:** at front, tele-hydraulic fork; at rear, swinging fork. **Wheels:** front 3.00×21, rear 4.75×18. **Brakes:** 160 mm front & rear. **Tank capcity:** 1.7 gallons. **Weight:** 211 lbs. **Performance:** not stated.

Manufacturer: Husqvarna Vapenfabriks, AB, Huskvarna

Monark 50 MX Formula (Morini)

Engine: 49 cc, single-cylinder two stroke, light alloy with chromium-plate linings. Bore and stroke: 38×42 mm. Compression ratio 12:1 Max. power 6.5 bhp at 9000 rpm. Dell'Orto carburettor. Bosch flywheel magneto ignition with external coil. **Transmission:** primary transmission by gears, secondary by non-enclosed chain drive. Multiple-disc clutch in oil bath. Five-speed gearbox. Kick start. **Frame:** duplex cradle. **Suspension:** at front, tele-hydraulic fork; at rear, swinging fork. **Wheels:** front 2.50×17, rear 3.00×16. **Brakes:** 115 mm front and rear. **Tank capacity:** 1.6 gallons. **Weight:** 143 lbs. **Performance:** not stated.

Manufacturer: MCB Monark, Crescent A.B., Box 141, Varberg

Monark 50 cc MX (Sachs)

Engine: 49 cc, single-cylinder two stroke, of light alloy with chromium-plated linings. Bore and stroke: 40×42 mm. Compression ratio not stated. Max. power not stated. Bing 27 mm carburettor. Bosch flywheel magneto ignition with Motoplat Thyristor external coil. **Transmission:** primary transmission by gears, secondary by non-enclosed chain drive. Multiple-disc clutch in oil bath. Six-speed gearbox. Kick start. **Frame:** duplex cradle. **Suspension:** at front, Ceriani tele-hydraulic fork; at rear, Girling swinging fork. **Wheels:** front 3.00×21, rear 3.50×18. **Brakes:** 120 mm front and rear. **Tank capacity:** not stated. **Weight:** 165 lbs. **Performance:** not stated.

Manufacturer: MCB Monark, Crescent A.B., Box 141, Varberg

Monark 125 TTS

Engine: 122 cc, single-cylinder two stroke; cylinder of light alloy with a large finning area and chromium-plated lining. Bore and stroke: 54×54 mm. Compression ratio 11.8:1. Max. power 17.6 bhp at 7500 rpm. Central Bing carburettor with 27 mm choke. Motoplat Thyristor 6V 35–5/21W ignition.

Transmission: primary transmission utilizes gears, secondary transmission utilizes semi-enclosed chain drive. Multiple-disc clutch in oil bath. Six-speed gearbox. Kick start.

Frame: duplex cradle.

Suspension: at front, tele-hydraulic fork; at rear, swinging fork.

Wheels: front 3.00×17, rear 3.50×17.

Brakes: 160 mm front and rear.

Tank capacity: 2.2 gallons.

Weight: 231 lbs.

Performance: max. speed approx. 74 mph.

Manufacturer: MCB Monark, Crescent A.B., Box 141, Varberg

Monark ISDT 125/175

Engine: 123(171) cc, single-cylinder, two stroke, light-alloy cylinder with chrome bore. Bore and stroke: 54×54(63.5×54) mm. Compression ratio and max. power not stated. 28(30) mm Bing carburettor. Motoplat Thyristor ignition.
Transmission: primary by gears, secondary by chain. Multiple-disc clutch in oil bath. Six-speed gearbox. Kick start.
Frame: duplex cradle.
Suspension: at front, tele-hydraulic fork; at rear, swinging fork.
Wheels: front 3.00×21, rear 4.25×18.
Brakes: 140 mm front, 120 mm rear.
Tank capacity: 1.6(1.9) gallons.
Weight: 209(215) lbs.
Performance: not stated.

Manufacturer: MCB Monark, Crescent A.B., Box 141, Varberg

Monark 125 TS

Engine: 123 cc, single-cylinder two stroke, light alloy cylinder with chrome bore. Bore and stroke: 54×54 mm. Compression ratio 11:1. Max. power 15 bhp at 7500 rpm. 27 mm Dell'Orto carburettor. Flywheel magneto ignition 6V/35W.
Transmission: primary by gears, secondary by chain. Multiple-disc clutch in oil bath. Five-speed gearbox. Kick start.
Frame: duplex cradle.
Suspension: at front, tele-hydraulic fork; at rear, swinging fork.
Wheels: front 3.00×17, rear 3.50×17.
Brakes: 140 mm front and rear.
Tank capacity: 2.2 gallons.
Weight: 231 lbs.
Performance: max. speed 71 mph.

Manufacturer: MCB Monark, Crescent A.B., Box 141, Varberg

AMF Harley-Davidson Sportster 1000 XL and XLCH

Engine: 997 cc, twin-cylinder four stroke engine arranged fore and aft. Overhead valve driven by rocker arms and push rods. Bore and stroke: 81×97 mm. Compression ratio 9:1. Max. power not stated. Bendix membrane carburettor. Forced lubrication. Flywheel ignition, alternator with 12V battery.
Transmission: primary transmission utilizes Triplex chain drive, secondary transmission utilizes single chain drive. Multiple-disc clutch in oil bath. Four-speed gearbox. Kick start for XLCH model, electric start for XL model.
Frame: duplex cradle.
Suspension: at front, telehydraulic fork; at rear, swinging fork.
Wheels: front 3.75×19, rear 4.25×18.
Brakes: front 292 mm disc, rear, 203 mm drum.
Tank capacity: 2 gallons.
Weight: 528 lbs.
Performance: max. speed approx. 108 mph.

Manufacturer: AMF Harley-Davidson, Milwaukee, Wisconsin 53201

AMF Harley-Davidson Super Glide 1200 FX and FXE

Engine: 1207 cc, twin-cylinder four stroke engine arranged fore and aft. Overhead valve driven by rocker arms and push rods. Bore and stroke: 87.3×100.8. Compression ratio 8:1. Max. power not stated. Bendix carburettor diameter 38 mm. Forced lubrication. Flywheel ignition, alternator with 12V battery.
Transmission: primary transmission utilizes dual chain drive, secondary transmission utilizes single chain drive. Dry multiple-disc clutch. Four-speed gearbox. Kick start for FX model, electric start for FXE model.
Frame: duplex cradle.
Suspension: at front, telehydraulic fork; at rear, swinging fork.
Wheels: front 3.75×19; rear 5.10×16.
Brakes: front 293 mm, rear 255 mm.
Tank capacity: 3.3 gallons.
Weight: 539 lbs.
Performance: max. speed 117 mph.

Manufacturer: AMF Harley-Davidson, Milwaukee, Wisconsin 53201

AMF Harley-Davidson Electra Glide FLH 1200

Engine: 1207 cc twin-cylinder 4 stroke engine arranged fore and aft. Overhead valve driven by rocker arms and push rods. Bore and stroke: 87.3×100.8 mm. Compression ratio 8:1. Max. power not stated. Bendix carburettor, diameter 38 mm. Forced lubrication. Flywheel ignition, alternator with 12V battery.

Transmission: primary transmission utilizes duplex chain drive, secondary transmission utilizes simplex chain drive. Dry multiple-disc clutch. Four-speed gearbox.

Frame: duplex cradle.

Suspension: at front, telehydraulic fork; at rear, swinging fork.

Wheels: front and rear, 5.10×16.

Brakes: 254 mm front and rear.

Tank capacity: 3.3 gallons (4.2 gallons on request).

Weight: 715 lbs.

Performance: max. speed approx. 111 mph.

Manufacturer: AMF Harley-Davidson, Milwaukee, Wisconsin 53201

Indian MS 175

Engine: 171 cc, single-cylinder two stroke with light alloy cylinder. Bore and stroke: 66×50 mm. Compression ratio 6.8:1. Max. power not stated. VM concentric carburettor with 26 mm choke. Flywheel magneto 6V/45W ignition.
Transmission: primary transmission utilizes gears, secondary transmission utilizes non-enclosed chain drive. Multiple-disc clutch in oil bath. Five-speed gearbox. Kick start.
Frame: duplex cradle.

Suspension: at front, telehydraulic fork; at rear, swinging fork.

Wheels: front 3.00×18, rear 3.50×17.

Brakes: 130 mm front and rear.

Tank capacity: 1.6 gallons.

Weight: 224 lbs.

Performance: max. speed not stated.

Manufacturer: The Indian Motorcycle Company, 110 North Dovery Street, Beverly Hills, California

Indian M1 175 A

Engine: 171 cc, single-cylinder two stroke with light alloy cylinder. Bore and stroke: 66×50 mm. Compression ratio 6.8:1. Max. power not stated. Central VM carburettor with 26 mm choke. Flywheel magneto 6V 33W ignition.

Transmission: primary transmission utilizes gears, secondary transmission utilizes semi-enclosed chain drive. Multiple-disc clutch in oil bath. Five-speed gearbox. Kick start.

Frame: duplex cradle.

Suspension: at front, telehydraulic fork; at rear, swinging fork.

Wheels: front 3.00×19, rear 4.00×17.

Brakes: 130 mm front and rear.

Tank capacity: 1.6 gallons.

Weight: 224 lbs.

Performance: max. speed not stated.

Manufacturer: The Indian Motorcycle Company, 110 North Dovery Street, Beverly Hills, California

Rokon RT-1

Engine: 335 cc, single-cylinder two stroke. Bore and stroke: 78×70 mm. Compression ratio 11.8:1. Max. power 37 bhp at 6500 rpm. 36 mm Mikuni carburettor. Ignition by flywheel magneto.
Transmission: primary transmission by gears, secondary by chain. Automatic transmission. Kick start.

Frame: duplex cradle.

Suspension: at front, telehydraulic fork, at rear, swinging fork.

Wheels: front 3.00×21, rear 4.00×18.

Brakes: 275 mm front and rear.

Tank capacity: 2.8 gallons.

Weight: 253 lbs.

Performance: max. speed 56 mph.

Manufacturer: Rokon Inc., 160 Emerald Street, Keene, N.H. 03431

Rokon MX 11

Engine: 335 cc, single cylinder two stroke producing 37 bhp at 6500 rpm. Bore and stroke: 78×70 mm. Compression ratio 11.8:1. Mikuni carburettor with 36 mm choke. Ignition by Bosch flywheel magneto.

Transmission: primary transmission by gears, secondary by chain. Automatic transmission. Kick start.

Frame: duplex cradle.

Suspension: at front, telehydraulic fork; at rear, swinging fork.

Wheels: front 3.00×21, rear 4.00×18.

Brakes: 275 mm front and rear.

Tank capacity: 1.5 gallons.

Weight: 253 lbs.

Performance: max. speed 56 mph.

Manufacturer: Rokon Inc., 160 Emerald Street, Keene, N.H. 03431

Cossack 650 D

Engine: 650 cc, twin-cylinder four stroke, horizontally opposed cylinders. Bore and stroke 78×68 mm. Compression ratio 7:1. Max. power 30 bhp at 5000 rpm. Two K302 carburettors. Forced lubrication. 6V/65W. electrical system. 6V battery.

Transmission: primary transmission utilizes gears, secondary transmission uses prop shaft and universal couplings. Dry, twin-plate clutch. Four-speed gearbox. Hand-operated reverse. Kick start.

Frame: duplex cradle.

Suspension: at front, telehydraulic fork; at rear, swinging fork with adjustable shock-absorbers.

Wheels: front and rear 3.75×19.

Brakes: 200 mm front and rear.

Tank capacity: 4.6 gallons.

Weight: 418 lbs.

Performance: max. speed approx. 83 mph.

Manufacturer: V/O Avtoexport, Smolenskaja-Sennaja Pl., 32/34, Moscow